Evidence of God

Evidence of God

A Scientific Case for God

NICK HAWKES

WIPF & STOCK · Eugene, Oregon

EVIDENCE OF GOD
A Scientific Case for God

Copyright © 2012 Nick Hawkes. All rights reserved. Except for brief quotations in critical publications or reviews, no part of this book may be reproduced in any manner without prior written permission from the publisher. Write: Permissions, Wipf and Stock Publishers, 199 W. 8th Ave., Suite 3, Eugene, OR 97401.

Wipf & Stock
An Imprint of Wipf and Stock Publishers
199 W. 8th Ave., Suite 3
Eugene, OR 97401
www.wipfandstock.com

ISBN 13: 978-1-62032-144-7

Manufactured in the U.S.A.

All scripture quotations, unless otherwise indicated, are taken from the Holy Bible, New International Version®, NIV®. Copyright ©1973, 1978, 1984 by Biblica, Inc.™ Used by permission of Zondervan. All rights reserved worldwide.

Previously published as: *The Dance Between Science and Faith: A Scientific Case for God*. Copyright © 2007 N. J. Hawkes Now updated and reprinted as *Evidence of God*

All cartoons provided courtesy of Patrick Atherton

*To my twin brother Tim Hawkes, who has shared
my life, my love, and my quest for truth.*

Contents

Foreword by Dr. Mark Worthing ix
Introduction xi

1. The Changing Relationship between Science and Christianity 1
2. Science Allows Faith 22
3. Cosmic Order as Evidence for God 52
4. Cosmic Disorder as Evidence against God 84
5. Theology Completes Science 100
6. Conclusion 124

Endnotes 135
Bibliography 161

Foreword

Nick Hawkes takes us on a journey through the history of the relationship between science and Christian faith in order to provide a better understanding of both science and faith. Along the way he introduces us to a number of key people and ideas who have helped to shape the current debate. Hawkes is a good guide for this journey. He knows the terrain well and is able to explain complex ideas in ordinary language. But most importantly, he knows where he is going. Keenly aware that science, in the popular imagination, is seen as standing in opposition to faith, he sets out to defend Christian belief. His defense, however, is not a call to arms against science, but an invitation to join science, properly understood, in a great cosmic dance of understanding.

The publishing of Richard Dawkins's *The God Delusion* is a potent reminder that, for many, the war between science and faith is far from over. Despite an explosion of literature exploring the possibilities for collaboration and cooperation between science and Christian faith in recent decades there persists within the community at large a perception that science and faith, and particularly Christian faith, are at odds. This leaves Christianity in a state of continued assault from those like Dawkins whose main arguments against the existence of God and the viability of Christian belief are ostensibly based upon modern science. All of this presents a particularly difficult task for the apologist, or defender of Christian belief. Certainly Dawkins and others of his ilk cannot be ignored, especially when some Christians are willing to agree with Dawkins that science and faith are essentially incompatible.

This is where Nick Hawkes's book takes up the challenge of the defense of Christian faith. He tackles popular perceptions about Christianity and science, for instance that Christianity has generally been anti-science, or that it is no longer credible in light of current scientific knowledge. Hawkes looks at science-based arguments for and against the existence for God and comes finally to the conclusion that faith can no more dispense with science than science can dispense with God. In doing this, Hawkes adopts an apologetic stance that sees him not only defending Christianity, rightly understood, but also science, rightly understood. Hawkes believes that true science, by its very nature, is no threat to Christianity and hence defends science before those Christians who would see science as the enemy. He also calls upon scientists to understand the true nature of their own discipline.

Hawkes's book makes much of the metaphor of the dance. The dance between science and faith seems at first like a dance between two very unlikely partners, but this is only if we persist with our misconceptions about both Christian faith and science. Regardless of how successful many theologians and scientists think they have been in the effort to bridge the gulf between these two great ways of making sense of the world, the data from studies of the views of the vast majority of those in our communities suggests that there has been little impact in terms of public perception. Hawkes provides us with a guide to bridging the gulf between Christian faith and science aimed at those who fight the battle for the popular imagination. The optimism that Hawkes has that both Christianity and science can be successfully defended and can thrive best when working cooperatively is seen not only in the image of the dance, but also in his careful and persuasive arguments throughout the book.

Hawkes concludes his book with the argument that Christian theology, rather than undermining science, actually provides science with a solid ground of meaning on which to stand. Science at the same time shows us the wonder of the one we worship as creator, even when its findings challenge long-held concepts about how God created, or how God acts in the world. The only satisfactory resolution for both science and theology, Hawkes argues, is when both realize that they complete one another. This is indeed a very welcome and positive basis upon which to defend the truth and power of Christian belief in an age of science.

Mark Worthing BA, Mdiv, STM, PhD, Dr Theol
(Dean of Studies, Tabor College, Adelaide, South Australia)
Dr Mark Worthing's Book, *God, Creation and Contemporary Physics*
won the John Templeton Prize in 1997.

Introduction

A YOUNG GRADUATE SAT opposite me, recalling her tears of frustration during her studies. She had been doing a unit in philosophy as part of her degree. Early on in this course, she was required to sit through a lecture on why God didn't exist. According to the lecturer, the existence of God was not scientifically credible. Objections to this teaching were met with derision.

It is indeed tragic when a university allows indoctrination to replace debate, simplistic parodies to replace truth, and inquiring minds to be shut down by humanist dogma. No search for truth, however inconvenient to our presuppositions, should be ridiculed.

What, then, can we know about the scientific credibility of faith? Is it true that "a scientific breakthrough a day will keep the need for God away"? Do we have to choose between faith and reason or can science and faith be mutually supportive?

I believe that science and theology are not inherently antagonistic toward each other but are compatible and can enrich each other. Many good reasons exist to challenge the perception that Christianity is not scientifically credible. Some of these reasons have only recently emerged as a result of recent scientific research. As such, we are now much better placed to answer the concern of Joseph Le Conte, Professor of Geology at the University of California, Berkeley, who wrote in 1902 that there was, "a constantly growing feeling amongst intelligent people, that there is an irreconcilable antagonism between science and revelation."[1]

There is little doubt that the Christian gospel is being hampered today by a perception that Christianity is antagonistic towards conventional science. Science is not seen as an area where Christianity can expect to have much input other than to stand against it with its own barely credible teaching. There is a perceived disparity between Christian dogma and the "pure" objective truth of science. The rift between the two disciplines is exacerbated by religious extremists who are antagonistic towards conventional science. This causes many to believe that the dead hand of religion is still trying to suppress the truth that was hard won and emancipated by the Enlightenment.

The "truth claims" of Christianity are also discordant to post-modern ears which are suspicious of any truth claim emanating from, what they believe to be, inherently repressive institutions. As such, a climate of suspicion regarding Christianity is all too prevalent, whether it arises from a modern or post-modern mindset. This is the reality which all Christians face in their ministry today. Questions about science and faith continually impinge on their ministry.

It has certainly impinged on mine. Some years ago, I was sacked as co-host of a Christian talk-back radio station for allowing that it was possible for people to be Christians yet not believe in six literal days of creation. I had said on air that many Christians understood the first three chapters of Genesis to be speaking about theology's "who" and "why" rather than science's "how" and "when." On another occasion, I received a call to come and speak to the Stirling Uniting Church's men's breakfast. The men there were unsure of what to believe as a result of hearing Sir Mark Oliphant, a retired eminent scientist (now deceased), give reasons why he, as a scientist, could not believe in God. Some weeks later, I had coffee with a retired research agriculturalist who asked me, with candid bewilderment, "How can you be a church minister if you are a scientist?" Months later, I was besieged with the same question by a group of educated young adults after conducting a wedding at which I had spoken briefly about having a faith that was scientifically reasonable. Questions about science have continually impinged on my ministry.

An examination of the books in the science section of many Australian Christian bookshops would justify people's expectation that most church ministers would be against conventional science.[2] In fact, the very preponderance of anti-evolution books has helped fuel a sub-culture amongst Christians that believes that good science has now discredited the evolution theory.[3] Such an understanding is, of course, not accorded any credibility by contemporary scientists who, by and large, find the theory of evolution to be a remarkably good model that helps explains how living things came to be as they are.

Further evidence of disagreement between Christianity and the scientific community was indicated by the 1991 Australian National Church Life Survey (NCLS) which reported that 51 percent of churchgoers did not believe in evolution.[4] The survey indicated that those holding a literalist biblical view of creation were more likely to be young, less educated and unlikely to belong to an Anglican or Uniting Church.[5] The attitude to evolution by these Christians is just one more factor that has helped people in Australia believe that the church is antagonistic towards science.

These results mirror those found in the rest of the Western world. A 1999 poll by the Gallup Organization asked people in the United States of America to say whether or not they believed, "God created humans in this present form within the past 10,000 years or so." This was the result:

- 55 percent of those with at least high school education said yes.
- 43 percent of those with at least some college education said yes.
- 39 percent of college graduates said yes.
- 28 percent of postgraduates/professors said yes.

These results tie in with the Australian National Church Life Survey (NCLS) that suggested that those holding to a literalist understanding of creation tended to have less formal education. However, this does not mean that educated scientists necessarily believe less than educated non-scientists. The Carnegie Commission surveyed over 60,000 scientific professors in the United States of America in 1969 and discovered that scientists attended church with the same regularity as the general population. They also discovered that social scientists (philosophers, psychologists and those teaching social work) were substantially less religious than those in the "hard" sciences such as maths, physics and life sciences.[7] As such, it is unwise to make generalizations about what scientists believe about God without taking into account their field of discipline.

Edward J. Larson and Larry Witham carried out a more recent study amongst American scientists in 1996. Their work revealed that 39 percent of scientists not only believed in a God but in a God to whom they could pray with the expectation of receiving an answer.[8] Interestingly, this statistic was not dissimilar to the 42 percent of scientists who responded in the same way when surveyed in 1914 by the American psychologist, James Leuba.[9] These results suggest that science does not inherently cause its acolytes to be less disposed to faith.

The physicist and theologian Robert Russell reminds us that, whilst it is important for Christians to show that faith is scientifically reasonable, the significance of science should not be overstated as a factor determining people's faith. He says, "For most people, faith does not come primarily from science or cosmology, or from philosophical arguments for the beginning of the world. It comes through the elemental religious experience of being encountered . . . by God."[10]

Nevertheless, whilst science may not be the major factor in determining what people believe, it nonetheless, remains an important factor. A British survey indicated that 22 percent of British people believe that science has explained life's mysteries,[11] suggesting that belief in God is not necessary.

Science matters because it impinges on our understanding of how God, if he exists, acts today. Can the hand of God be seen in science? Is humanity purposed by God or are we simply the product of blind happen-stance, the mechanism of which God has imbued in the physical laws of the universe?

Questions that frequently arise in ministry are: Does God push the start button and then withdraw with curiosity wondering what the universe will produce? Is God following a blueprint or is humanity the winner of a monstrous game of luck? If God is following a blueprint and we cannot change the course of events through our prayers, how can we have an authentic loving friendship with a God who is unable to respond? Is God distant, weak, evil or fictitious? These questions show that the issues surrounding science impinge on the very nature of our understanding of God, and are therefore of key importance.

A questionnaire was conducted amongst 390 tertiary trained people in South Australia in 2002.[12] Of these, 311 were classed as non-church attenders.[13] An analysis of their replies indicated that Christians seeking to engage non-church attenders in debate over the scientific credibility of faith, need to address four issues. The first of these is the perception that Christianity has generally been anti-science throughout history. The second is that Christianity is not credible in the light of scientific discoveries. The third is the issue of whether or not the order we see in creation points to the existence of God. The final issue is whether or not the chaos and suffering we see in the universe is evidence that a loving God does not exist.

The response Christians can give to these four key issues is the subject of this book.

1

The Changing Relationship Between Science and Christianity

*I have never been an atheist
in the sense of denying the existence of God.*

—CHARLES DARWIN (1879)[1]

SCIENCE'S DANCE WITH CHRISTIANITY has certainly been ambiguous, being sometimes a waltz (in beautiful harmony, being mutually supportive), a tango (treating the parter with disdain), and sometimes solo disco dancing (ignoring the other completely). This chapter explores how the relationship between science and Christianity has continually changed throughout history.

Science has not steadily diverged from theology. This fact is not widely appreciated. The results of the questionnaire conducted amongst 311 tertiary trained people in South Australia showed that 70 percent of non-church goers believe Christianity has generally been antagonistic towards science throughout history.[2] This result was consistent over different age groups and the subject areas people were trained in.

Clearly, many people believe that Christianity has been systemically anti-science throughout history. This mindset has gained momentum in the last two centuries, encouraged by works such as John Draper's *History of the Conflict between Religion and Science* (1875) and Andrew White's *A History of the Warfare of Science with Theology in Christendom* (1895) and, in more recent times, the writings of the biologist Richard Dawkins.[3] These have encouraged the idea that as science has grown in stature, it has increasingly shown Christian faith to be insupportable. We need to ask, is this understanding valid?

A right understanding of the relationship between science and theology today will require a right understanding of the history of the relationship between the two disciplines. When this is understood, it will become apparent that the relationship between science and Christianity has been a changing one that has alternated between being supportive and being antagonistic throughout the course of history. There is, therefore, no gradual, linear divergence of science from religion. In fact, cooperation between the two disciplines of science and theology is currently enjoying a renaissance.

THE EARLY SEARCH FOR FOUNDATIONAL VALUES: SCIENCE NURTURED BY THEOLOGY

To begin, it is perhaps important to remember that the way Christians think is a way remarkably conducive to the development of science. The physicist and theologian John Polkinghorne suggests three reasons why monotheistic faiths have encouraged science to flourish in a way it could not have done under ancient Greek or Chinese culture. Firstly, such a faith expects creation to be orderly because its Creator is rational. Observation and experiment are therefore indispensable tools in learning about God's created order. Secondly, because it is God's creation, it is worthy of study. Thirdly, because creation is not itself divine, we are at liberty to investigate it without impiety.

Polkinghorne may be being a little unkind to Greek and Chinese culture as Greek rationalism is very consistent with some aspects of modern science and the Chinese culture gave rise to new technologies well before they were developed in Europe. However, whilst the Chinese developed gunpowder, the magnetic compass and the printing press, it was not until they were adopted in Europe that their potential was greatly developed. This development was encouraged by the Christian understanding that humankind was significant and was able to take charge of its own destiny. European scientific curiosity had also been encouraged by the theology of Aquinas who promoted the idea that nature was worthy of examination in that it reflected aspects of God's glory. Later in history, the Reformation ensured that scientific discoveries were developed with the energy of the Protestant work ethic, the lack of which had stinted the development of scientific discoveries by the ancient Greeks who saw manual labor as demeaning because it created ties of dependence and was associated with slaves. The one exception the Greeks made was the labor associated with agriculture.[4]

Although Christianity is not inherently anti-science, Christians have struggled to understand how their faith should relate to science, particularly as the discipline of science grew through history. A key issue that was to emerge was the issue of how to understand biblical hermeneutics (how to interpret the Bible). In 415 AD, Augustine completed his commentary on Genesis, *De Genesi ad litteram*, in which he attempted to do justice to the scientific knowledge of his day. To do so, he felt it was necessary to treat some sections of Genesis metaphorically. His approach was to adopt a literal understanding of a Scriptural passage unless it could be established without doubt that a metaphorical reading was necessary.[5] He was also critical of those who turned to the Scriptures for answers to cosmological questions.

Whilst he held these views he would not, however, countenance any attack by science on the central principles of faith. He wrote:

> What is it to me whether the heavens like a sphere surround the earth or whether they cover the earth as would a disc over it? . . . the Spirit of God . . . did not wish to teach men things of no relevance to their salvation . . . We must show our Scriptures not to be in conflict with whatever (our critics) can demonstrate about the nature of things from reliable sources . . . but whatever in their books they put forward as contradicting the Scriptures, that is, the Catholic faith, we should either by some means show, or else unhesitatingly believe, to be most false.[6]

It is interesting that although Augustine was no scientist, he came to a conclusion about time that was proved to be remarkably consistent with Einstein's theory of relativity fifteen centuries later. He spoke of creation being a single timeless act through which time itself came to be.[7] Time was linear, not cyclical. This was contrary to the view of Aristotle (the fourth century BC philosopher) who argued that matter and time could have no beginning. This difference in understanding became a key point of debate amongst Christians as they explored the acceptability of Aristotelian physics to the believer.[8] As it has turned out, it would seem that Aristotle, the rationalist, may not have been as right about time as Augustine, the theologian.[9] The discovery of the second law of thermodynamics[10] and the credible theory of the "Big Bang" made the Aristotelian view of the cosmos implausible.

Having said this, it would be unwise to believe that the Aristotelian view has been completely discredited as theories akin to the Aristotelian view have continued to emerge even in recent years. For example, in 1950 Fred Hoyle published an idea first put forward by Hermann Bondi and Thomas Gold in 1948 that the universe had always been in a "steady state," neither expanding or contracting.[11] Although this idea was subsequently discredited, some have recently returned to an idea not unlike it as they explore the concept of there being a infinite number of universes or a universe that continually expands and contracts. This will be explored later.

Another contribution Augustine made that was helpful to science was his belief that the seeds of everything that would ever develop (stars, water, earth, and life) were placed in the universe by God and would only come into being when the right "causal connections," i.e., conditions, came about.[12] By allowing that everything was present in potential seed form, Augustine allowed for a developmental process in creation.

Of particular benefit to science was Augustine's warning against reading Scripture as a straight-jacketed understanding of cosmology. He correctly anticipated the change and development of scientific theory and stressed the importance of not tying science down to a particular theological world view.[13] In doing this, Augustine gave science a theological freedom to develop.

In Western Christendom, the thirteenth century scholar Thomas Aquinas (c.1225–1274) gave clear expression of the conviction that creation's order pointed to God's existence. His was an "argument from design," sometimes called a "teleological argument" (an argument directed toward some end). Thomas expressed his thinking in his "Five Ways," his five arguments for God's existence. In summary, these were:

1. The world is in motion and is continually changing. It is not static but dynamic. God must be directing it.

2. Everything is determined by cause and effect. The ultimate cause must be God.

3. Unnecessary beings exist. The fact that we are here needs explanation.

4. Where do the values of truth, goodness and nobility come from if they do not come from God?

5. There is evidence of intelligent design in creation.[14]

Although Thomas' principles have since been challenged, aspects of his thinking have proven resilient and are discernible in modern day apologetics, e.g., of John Polkinghorne who advocates the reasonableness of faith in the light of scientific evidence. Thomas' other genius was that by not tying theology too closely to science, he, like Augustine, gave room for science to develop without it threatening the overall, consistent principles of Scripture.[15] This is significant. If Scripture had tied its understanding too closely to contemporary science, it would have had to continually revise its theology to keep current with scientific advances. As it is, Christian theology hangs more loosely with science, allowing the consistent principles of Scripture, conceived in the bronze age, to speak the same changeless truth to the space age.

COPERNICUS AND GALILEO: THEOLOGY'S SUPPRESSION OF SCIENCE

It can be said that, to this point in medieval history, there were no deep rifts between science and theology and their relationship was generally harmonious. This relationship was to be challenged, however, by the scientific discoveries in astronomy of Nicholas Copernicus (1473–1543) and Galileo Galilei (1564–1642).[16] Notwithstanding this challenge, it must be remembered that most early scientists were deeply religious people. Copernicus, for example, was a minor church official.

Three factors need to be appreciated if the struggle between science and religion in the next three centuries is to be understood. The first of these was the battle for power and influence. Any possibility of the church accepting scientific evidence as truth largely became a casualty of the church's desire to maintain control and right order in times of schism. However, the church's rejection of Copernicus' ideas was by no means universal. The Carmelite friar, Paolo Antonio Foscarini (1580–1616), wrote to Cardinal Bellarmine in 1615 saying that he believed that Copernicus' heliocentric model of the cosmos (that the earth was not the center of the universe but revolved around the sun) was not inconsistent with the Bible.[17] He claimed that if Scripture says something incommensurate with science, Scripture was :

1. speaking metaphorically with similitude; or
2. speaking in a mode that was accommodated to our understanding; or
3. speaking in a common colloquial fashion.[18]

Cardinal Robert Bellarmine was Professor of Controversial Theology (1576–1594) and Rector of the Roman College (1592–1594) before being made Cardinal. He was later to play a key role in the Counter Reformation and in the proceedings that led to the Catholic Church's condemnation of Copernicanism in 1616. It is significant that Copernican astronomy was not Bellarmine's area of competence but his personal authority was such that his opposition to Copernican ideas (expressed in his reply to Foscarini) led to Foscarini's letter being "altogether prohibited and damned."[19]

In passing, it is worth noting that there is a popular misconception that Copernicus held back publication of his *De Revolutionibus* until after his death out of fear of persecution by the church. This was not the case as he had outlined his heliocentric theory before his death in *Commentariolus,* a forty page summary of his ideas which he gave to friends and colleagues. In fact, the University of Wittenberg (where Martin Luther was teaching) and Cardinal Schönberg both urged Copernicus to publish his theory in more detail so it could be studied.[20]

Another myth that should perhaps be debunked is that when Galileo invited contemporary academics to look through his telescope (so they could see evidence for his theories in the night sky) the theologians refused. In writing to his friend, the German astronomer, Johannes Kepler, in 1610, Galileo was indeed scornful of those who refused to look through his telescope. However, those that refused were philosophers (whom later historians identified as Cesare Cremonini and Giulio Libria). As far as we can tell, the theologians all took a look.

It should be remembered that during the time of Cardinal Bellarmine, the church was not primarily concerned with physical cosmologies or world-views but was keenly aware of its need to declare the Church's authority in interpreting the Bible. This was because the Reformation had emancipated the Bible from the hands of clerics and made it available to the laity. This challenged the authority of the Catholic clerics. The issue at stake was therefore not so much cosmological truth as right order and control.[21]

Galileo Galilei developed Copernicus' ideas further, expressing his conviction that they were true in his Letter to the Grand Duchess Christina in 1615. However, notwithstanding his Copernican ideas, Galileo retained a high view of Scripture and made it clear that he, like Augustine, believed that anything attacking holy Scriptures must be treated as false.[22] He understood Scripture to be neutral regarding cosmology, saying: "if the Holy Spirit has purposely neglected to teach us propositions of this sort as irrelevant to (salvation), how can anyone affirm that it is obligatory to take side on them?"[23]

Galileo argued that there were instances where:

1. the Bible spoke metaphorically (as when attributing human features to God);
2. the biblical authors accommodated their language to the understanding of the common people;
3. the biblical author's concern was helping people attain salvation, not teaching cosmology.[24]

It is pertinent to note that Cardinal Maffeo Barberini (who became Pope Urban VIII who later presided over Galileo's trial), was initially a friend and admirer of Galileo and listened to his theories with sympathy and even benevolence. Galileo knew Barberini was not wanting to frustrate the development of science,[25] he was simply someone who believed that no mathematical theory could fully unlock the secrets of how the universe moved.[26] It must be remembered that this was an age in which science was not accorded much significance. Astronomy and mathematics were considered as the play things of virtuosi and were not considered to have much philosophical or theological significance.

School was different in Galileo's time!

This highlights the second factor that helped develop a rift between science and faith. This was the technical inability of the clerics in power to fully understand complex mathematical arguments of astronomy and appreciate the compelling nature of its arguments.

The church's lack of sympathy for Galileo's science was not helped by Galileo falling from the Pope's favor as a result of some insensitive political moves by Galileo and his supporters. One of his most unwise moves was to put the Pope's arguments against Galileo's theory in the mouth of the fool, Simplicius, in his book, *Dialogue Concerning the Two Chief World Systems—Ptolemaic and Copernican*.[27] One way or another, things came to a head and Galileo was brought to trial on the 22nd of June, 1633, after which he was required, under threat of torture, to "abjure, curse and detest" his Copernican theories.[28]

The third major factor to exacerbate the rift between science and faith was an inadequate understanding of Biblical authority. Behind much of the debate about science's relationship with faith was a genuine quest to uncover how the Scriptures were authoritative for faith. The concern of the church was for biblical faithfulness.[29]

THE REFORMATION AND BIBLICAL AUTHORITY: SCIENCE'S AMBIGUOUS RELATIONSHIP WITH THEOLOGY

Broadly speaking, there have been three approaches to understanding Biblical authority in history. The first has been the "literal" approach that believes, for example, that the first three chapters of Genesis are scientifically true. The second has been the "allegorical" approach, popularized by Origen (the second century Alexandrian Christian theologian) which did not treat the Bible as a literal historical account but as a poetic or allegorical teaching. Thirdly, there has been the "accommodation" approach. This taught that revelation takes place in a culturally, human centered manner. Key truths have been accommodated to the culture of the time. This understanding was influential during the patristic period and gained great momentum in the sixteenth century.[30] It was an approach that gave room for science to live comfortably with theology. Nevertheless, the accommodation theory has never held complete sway, and this has meant that science's relationship with theology was never uniformly the same throughout Christendom from the time of the Reformation, through the Enlightenment, until today.

John Calvin was one who gave impetus to the accommodation approach and, in doing so, helped to eliminate the significant obstacle of biblical literalism to the development of science. When discussing why God should reveal to us in Scripture that creation took six days, Calvin says, "Let us rather conclude that God himself took the space of six days, for the purpose of accommodating his works to the capacity of men."[31] Calvin pointed out that the Bible is primarily concerned with the knowledge of Jesus Christ.[32] It is not a scientific textbook. God has to come down to our level to reveal himself but has needed to accommodate his language to meet our limited abilities and understandings.[33] Calvin says: "He who would learn astronomy and other recondite arts, let him go elsewhere."[34] He explains that when the author of Genesis described the waters above and below the earth, he did so in order that "the rude and unlearned may perceive."[35] He believed that God "did not treat the stars scientifically, like a philosopher" in Scripture[36] and therefore felt free to defend astronomy saying, "Nevertheless, this study is not to be reprobated, nor this science to be condemned, because some frantic persons are wont boldly to reject whatever is unknown to them."[37]

Later, in speaking about Psalm 19, Calvin introduces the idea of metaphor and says, "David here metaphorically introduces the splendor and magnificence of the heavenly bodies"[38] and goes on to say, "It would have been lost time for David to have attempted to teach the secrets of astronomy to the rude and unlearned; and therefore he reckoned it sufficient to speak in a homely style."[39]

However, Calvin's understanding was not universal at the time of the Reformation. Luther was more literal in his understanding. A celebrated example of this occurred in his debate with Zwingli over the interpretation of Matthew 26:26, "This is my body." Luther argued that the "is" must be taken literally.[40] Luther was dismissive of Copernicus' theory, writing (with reference to Joshua 10:12), that Joshua commanded the sun not the earth to stand still.[41] However, Luther may not have held his anti-Copernican views very strongly. One of Copernicus' earliest adherents, Erasmus Reinhold, was permitted to teach in Wittenburg at Luther's side without any problems. This leads Heinrich Bornkamm to say that: "Luther . . . did not interfere with the freedom of the new knowledge in the field of science."[42] Bornkamm is perhaps being a little generous. Luther was not indifferent to Copernicus' theory and Luther's literal understanding of Joshua 10:12 would have given support to the biblical literalists. Luther was not, however, always consistent. Whilst he could say that Scripture had never erred, he could nonetheless also say, "When one reads (in the Bible) that great numbers of people were slain —for example eighty thousand—I believe that hardly one thousand were actually killed. What is meant is the whole people."[43] Clearly, Luther did not see mathematical precision as the point at issue.

Whilst a key concern for Luther was the right understanding of biblical authority, he also applauded the study of nature, for he saw in nature powerful evidence of God's existence and character. He wrote, "All creation is the most beautiful book or Bible; in it God has described and portrayed Himself."[44] Luther was therefore not anti-intellectual. He wrote that any interested person could see that there was "much secret activity in nature" and whoever was able to apply the understandings nature taught seem to be performing miracles in the eyes of those who did not possess such knowledge.[45]

Notwithstanding some points of similarity, Calvin and Luther's approach to Scripture and science were clearly not the same. This indicates that not only could science's relationship with religion vary and change with time but that there can also be variations within the same time—as indeed is the case today.

THE TWO BOOKS OF REVELATION: SCIENCE SUPPORTIVE OF THEOLOGY

Following this period of history, the relationship between science and theology began to heal and become mutually supportive of each other. This happened particularly in England during the seventeenth and eighteenth century. The reason for this was a growing conviction that understanding the design and complexity of nature helped lay bare the glories of God's handiwork. In studying nature, scientists felt they were following a biblical mandate to display the evidence of God in creation. This was consistent with biblical teaching:

> The heavens are telling the glory of God, and the firmament proclaims his handiwork. (Psalm 19:1)

> God's eternal power and divine nature . . . have been understood and seen through the things he has made. (Romans 1:20)

This understanding gave rise to "natural theology" which saw God's eloquent self-revelation in creation.

The idea of complementarity between natural and revealed theology was not new. It had been an understanding promoted by the early Church Father, Tertullian (155/60–220) who said, We maintain that God must first be known from nature, and afterwards authenticated by instruction: from nature by His works; by instruction, through His revealed announcements.[46]

Although the idea of God being known in the book of nature was a sound one, it did, sadly, have the unfortunate effect of making it easier for Stoic monism to infect Christian theology.[47] It encouraged the idea that nature had a personal identity and was set in place by God to govern the world whilst he withdrew to heaven.[48] This idea was popular during the twelfth century in circles connected with the school of Chatres and resurfaced continually throughout history, being seen today in those pantheistic philosophies which accord nature a personal identity. It was also to influence Newton in the seventeenth century.[49]

Isaac Newton (1642–1727) had a mechanistic world-view. He believed that the solar system operated according to definite inherent universal principles. God had made the universe like a clock which must work its inevitable self-governing way. God was hardly needed to make it work beyond creating the mechanism.[50] This was essentially a Deistic understanding. Deists believe in a benevolent but remote God whose concern is creation rather than salvation. They teach that God acts solely through the laws of nature. This understanding allows natural theology to become synonymous with natural religion. The German philosopher Gottfried Whilhelm Leibniz wrote of Newton, "Mr. Newton and his followers have an extremely odd opinion of the work of God . . . This God will be very like the Stoic God, who was the whole universe."[51] For all that, Isaac Newton saw his scientific work as helping people find faith. He wrote, "When I wrote my treatise about our system, I had an eye upon such principles as might work with considering men for the belief of a Deity."[52]

Earlier, John Calvin helped motivate scientific investigation by saying that it was a means of discerning the hand of God in creation. Nature is "before our eyes as a most beautiful book in which all created things, whether great or small, are as letters showing the invisible things of God to us."[53] He went on to say that Christians have an obligation to understand nature, saying, "If the Lord has been pleased to assist us by the work and ministry of the ungodly in physics, dialectics, mathematics and other similar sciences, let us avail ourselves of it, lest, by neglecting the gifts of God spontaneously offered to us, we be justly punished for our sloth."[54] However, Calvin was another that did not see the study of science and the study of the Bible as equal partners. He believed the Bible was needed to correct the imperfect understandings gleaned from nature.[55]

This growing appreciation of the wonders and design of nature gave rise to the notion of there being "two books" of revelation, the Book of the Bible and the Book of Nature. The seventeenth century father of scientific reasoning, Francis Bacon (1643–1727), was one who particularly popularized this idea, (sometimes known as the "Baconian compromise").[56] Bacon said that no one "can search too far, or be too well studied in the book of God's word, or in the book of God's works . . . but rather, let people endeavor an endless proficience in both." Charles Darwin was later to pen this quote opposite the title page in the preface of his book On the Origin of Species.[57] Bacon, nonetheless went on to caution that people should "not unwisely mingle or confound these learnings together."[58]

Thomas Brown, physician and author (1605–1682) was another who was convinced of the veracity of both the Bible and nature in revealing God. He wrote, "Thus are there two books from whence I collect my divinity: besides that written one of God, another of his servant nature, that universal and publick manuscript, that lies expansed to the eyes of all. Those that never saw him in the one have discovered him in the other."[59]

The scientific revolution of the sixteenth and seventeenth centuries fostered a sense of wonder at creation which helped reinforce the idea that study of the natural world glorified God. Robert Boyle wrote, "When with bold telescopes I survey the old and newly discovered stars and planets . . . when with excellent microscopes I discern nature's curious workmanship, when with the help of anatomical knives and the light of chemical furnaces I study the book of nature . . . I find myself exclaiming with the psalmist, 'How manifold are thy works, O God, in wisdom hast thou made them all!'[60] Boyle, therefore, celebrated the two disciplines of science and theology, declaring, "as the two great books of nature and Scripture have the same author, so the study of the latter does not at all hinder the inquisitive man's delight in the study of the former."[61] This conviction also led Boyle to bequeath money to fund the annual Boyle lectures for proving the truth of the Christian faith using the "argument from design."

The development of the argument from design perhaps found its finest expression in William Paley. His simple argument was that, "There cannot be design without a designer; contrivance without a contriver . . . The marks of design are too strong to be got over. Design must have had a designer. That designer must have been a person. That person is GOD."[62]

His book *Natural Theology; or Evidences of the Existence and Attributes of the Deity, Collected from the Appearances of Nature* (1802) developed the Deistic clockwork universe of Newton into an object of marvel, its mechanism being evidence for God.

> In crossing a heath, suppose I pitched my foot against a stone, and were asked how the stone came to be there. I might possibly answer, that . . . it had lain there for ever . . . But suppose I had found a watch . . . there must have existed, at some time and at some place or other, an artificer or artificers who formed it for the purpose which we find it actually to answer, who comprehended its construction and designed its use.[63]

Paley's reasoning was reflected in the *Bridgewater Treatises* (published between 1833 and 1840) produced by the bequest of the Eighth Earl of Bridgewater who funded eight treatise by different authors, all of whom wrote on evidence for God in creation. Nevertheless, this argument from design was not without its critics. It received criticism because of its insensitivity to the poor and suffering. By insisting that all development was by God's direct action, the plight of the suffering could be said to be purposed by God.[64] Despite this, the idea that the ordered designs seen in nature were evidence of God working out his purposes helped fuel a zeal for scientific research that included many nineteenth century clerics.

The two book metaphor is now generally on the wane, although it is still propounded in creationist circles and has made a recent resurgence with the "intelligent design" debate.[65] The Oxford philosopher and theologian Peter Hess, believes that two factors have helped its demise. The first was the advent of the printing press. The very accessibility of the Bible meant that it lost some of its special sacred status in the minds of the populace. The second was a growing understanding that species do not last forever. They become extinct. The apparent meaningless extinction of species, coupled with the suffering seen in nature meant that the finger of God was not at all obvious. As such, the book of nature was flawed.[66]

The most powerful challenge to the "argument from design," however, was to come from Charles Darwin.

DARWIN: SCIENCE'S GREATEST CHALLENGE TO THEOLOGY

Charles Darwin was a particularly key figure who influenced the history of the relationship between science and theology. His thinking challenged the understanding that the intricate designs seen in nature were evidence of God's handiwork. Paley could be believed until Darwin showed that "natural selection" could develop the design of a species over time. The hand of God was therefore not necessary. "From the war of nature . . . the production of the higher animals directly follows."[67] This understanding shattered the cosy relationship that had developed in England between science and faith.

It is important for the apologist to understand not only what Darwin said but the factors that led up to him saying them, otherwise it could be tempting to equate Darwin's loss of Christian faith[68] solely to the incompatibility of his scientific findings with faith, which would not be true.

Darwin went up to Cambridge in 1827 to train for the church at Christ's College, not for reasons of conviction but at his father's insistence. He also did so for reasons of expediency, seeing ordination into the Anglican church as a respectable profession which would allow him time to indulge in his other interests of shooting and being a naturalist.[69] He was, however, conscientious enough to do some study and read, amongst other things, the work of the apologist Rev. John Bird Sumner *The Evidence of Christianity derived from its natures and reception* (1821) which prompted Darwin to say that there was "no other way except by (Jesus') divinity" . . . of explaining existence. Christianity therefore remained "wonderfully suitable . . . to our ideas of happiness in this and the next world."[70] At this time, Darwin also held Paley's *Evidences of Christianity* in high regard.[71] In fact, it so delighted him that he learnt his arguments by heart even when many ordained Anglican dons at Cambridge considered them to be dangerously simplistic.[72]

Nevertheless, Darwin's brief grounding in Christianity was not enough to weather the trials of life or the discoveries he made. He came to disbelieve in Christianity as divine revelation.[73] Darwin was later to reflect on his brief period of faith and say "I did not then in the least doubt the strict and literal truth of every word in the Bible."[74] He recalled wryly the times he had been ridiculed by his shipmates for quoting Scripture early on during his voyage in the *Beagle*.[75] He wrote later, "Considering how fiercely I have been attacked by the orthodox it seems ludicrous that I once intended to be a clergyman."[76]

What factors caused Darwin to lose his faith? Four can be identified. The first was his upbringing. Darwin was brought up in a non-conformist, Unitarian environment. His two grandfathers were Josiah Wedgwood, a Unitarian, and Erasmus Darwin, a strident, even notorious, free thinker. Darwin's thinking was further shaped by his naturalist friend and freethinker, Robert Grant, during Darwins' failed attempt to study medicine at Edinburgh University.[77]

Secondly, his scientific discoveries pointed him towards a theory of natural selection that accounted for the increased complexity of life (and its apparent design) without invoking God. Darwin's theory of evolution through natural selection states that variations can occur in an organism that can confer a competitive advantage over other individuals of the species.[78] These new variations are selected by environmental pressures. Those organisms that are better able to survive because of these variations increase in number, and pass the helpful variation on to the following generations. This process results in organisms continually evolving and adapting to their ecological niches. Therefore, there is no divine plan, only a continuous process of blind adaptation or evolution.

The significance of Darwin's theory of evolution meant that God was no longer necessary to explain the complexity and design seen in nature. This impacted on Darwin's own faith. He wrote: "The old argument of design in nature, as given by Paley, which formally seemed to me so conclusive, fails now that the law of natural selection has been discovered."[79]

Thirdly, Darwin's observations on the suffering and cruelty of life were also an important factor causing him to lose faith in a beneficent God. Whilst Darwin found himself both in awe at the wonder and beauty of nature he also observed, as Alfred Tennyson said, that nature was "red in tooth and claw."[80] Darwin was repelled at the idea that a beneficent God could conceive of organisms such as the ichneumon wasp. This wasp has a long needle-like ovipositer protruding from its abdomen which it uses to inject its eggs into the bodies of living caterpillars. The ichneumon wasp larvae hatch and eat their way through the body of the caterpillar, eventually killing it.[81] He wrote to his friend and fellow naturalist Joseph Hooker and said, "I can see no evidence of beneficent design, or indeed design of any kind in the details."[82] Darwin's loss of faith in the Christian God of love also had much to do with the death of his beloved eldest child, Annie in 1851 when she was twelve years old. Her death shattered him and he grieved for her throughout his entire life.[83]

Fourthly, Darwin's loss of faith was influenced by the death of his non-Christian father in 1841 and his inability to accommodate the belief that the unsaved would go to hell. He wrote, "I can indeed hardly see how anyone ought to wish Christianity to be true; for if so, the plain language of the text seems to show that the men who do not believe, and this would include my father, brother and almost all my best friends, will be everlastingly punished. And this is a damnable doctrine."[84]

Darwin's convictions, understandably, caused him to be pilloried by many in the church. However, this was not universally so. He had, in fact, always valued the friendship and support of some Christian scholars and held his mentor, the eminent botanist and mineralogist, Rev. Professor J. S. Henslow, in the highest regard during his time in Cambridge and throughout his voyaging.[85] Later, he developed a lifelong friendship with The Rev. John Brodie Innes, a high churchman who became his confidant despite their different views.[86] He also enjoyed support from the country rector and novelist Charles Kingsley and the Harvard botanist, Professor Asa Gray, who both maintained that evolution was not incompatible with theism.[87] Kingsley wrote that he found it "just as noble a conception of Deity to believe that He created primal forms capable of self development."[88] Darwin was so delighted with this response and slipped these lines into the last chapter of the second edition of *Origins*, attributing them to "a celebrated author and divine."

It is also tempting to overplay the humiliation of the church in the form of Samuel Wilberforce, Bishop of Oxford, when he debated with Thomas Huxley and Joseph Hooker at a meeting of the British Association at Oxford on 30th June, 1860. In fact, the protagonists in the debate were not even the main billing for that night. The main speaker was Professor John Draper from New York University who gave a boring speech expounding aspects of Darwin's theory. Wilberforce had tried to lighten the proceedings by turning to Huxley and asking whether it was on his grandfather's or grandmother's side that he was descended from an ape - a statement which Huxley savaged.[89] This exchange has been inflated to the point of legend by supporters of Huxley, even though its impact was so minimal at the time that no mention was made of it in any publication for twenty years. It was only later that triumphalist accounts of the debate in support of Huxley began to appear, including a very uncomplimentary one about Wilberforce from Mrs Isabella Sidgewick which was published in *Macmillan's Magazine*. Her view belied the fact that Wilberforce had always thought Darwin to be a "capital fellow"[90] (despite his dismay at Darwin's evolutionary ideas) and that he had written an extensive review of *Origin of Species* which Darwin regarded as significant enough to cause him to modify his discussion at several points.[91] It is also worth noting that the day after Huxley and Hooker's celebrated debate with Wilberforce, Frederick Temple (the future Archbishop of Canterbury) preached that the finger of God could be seen at work in the laws of nature. He said that religious apologists had too often tried to make capital out of scientific ignorance and that there was no need to oppose the extension of natural law into new territory.[92] It is, in fact, significant that Darwin's theory was generally accepted quite quickly by the main line denominations of the Christian church.

Whilst it is important to correct erroneous folklore about Darwin, it would be unfair to say that Darwin's thinking did not cause great debate or incur a savage reaction from many in the church. Previously, humanity was sharply distinguished from the rest of nature, but since Darwin, humanity has been understood to be part of nature, the product of a common evolutionary heritage.[93] The Darwinian theory loosened the knot that tied humankind from other life forms. As the physicist and cosmologist Paul Davies says, people "were no longer cast at the center of the great scheme, but were relegated to an incidental and seemingly pointless role in an indifferent cosmic drama, like unscripted extras that have accidentally stumbled onto a vast movie set."[94]

What did Darwin believe about design and purpose? Darwin never denied design but believed it was due to natural selection. He believed that the universe existed because of designed law but that the details were left to chance. However, he was uncertain whether or not the laws of natural selection had their origin in a greater cause which was directing existence to some purpose. Darwin was never to lose entirely his belief in divine providence.

> the birth both of the species and of the individual are equally parts of that grand sequence of events, which our minds refuse to accept as the result of blind chance. The understanding revolts at such a conclusion, whether or not we are able to believe that every slight variation of structure . . . and other such events, have all been ordained for some special purpose.[95]

Darwin had known enormous feelings of awe akin to religious experiences when contemplating the grandeur of nature and spoke of his soul responding to nature's God. He had written: "In my Journal, I wrote that whilst standing in the midst of the grandeur of a Brazilian forest, 'it is not possible to give an adequate idea of the higher feelings of wonder, admiration and devotion which fill and elevate the mind."[96] However, Darwin later became convinced that these splendors could "hardly be advanced as an argument for the existence of God."[97]

Despite this, Darwin could not reconcile to himself the idea that humankind was meaningless. He believed that humanity would continue to develop and become more perfect. For him, it was "an intolerable thought that he and all other sentient beings are doomed to complete annihilation after such long continued slow progress."[98] Darwin continually struggled with:

> The impossibility of conceiving this immense and wonderful universe, including man . . . as the result of blind chance or necessity. When thus reflecting I feel compelled to look to a First Cause having an intelligent mind in some degree analogous to that of man and I deserve to be called a Theist. But then arises the doubt, can the mind of man, which has, as I fully believe, been developed from a mind as low as that possessed by the lowest animal, be trusted when it draws such grand conclusions.[99]

Even though Darwin was always to struggle with the idea of divine providence, he felt certain enough to write in 1879 "I have never been an Atheist in the sense of denying the existence of God," but that as he grew older, he said that "an agnostic would be the more correct description of my state of mind."[100] He believed that the philosophy of nature he was discovering pointed to the grandeur of a deity. In the final pages of *The Origin of Species* he speaks of "the laws impressed on matter by the Creator"[101] and goes on to end his book by saying:

> There is a grandeur in this view of life, which its several powers, having been originally breathed into a few forms or into one; and that, whilst this planet has gone cycling on according to the fixed law of gravity, from so simple a beginning endless forms most beautiful and most wonderful have been, and are being, evolved.[102]

How should we respond to Darwin? A well considered contemporary response to Darwin was made by Charles Hodge of Princeton Theological Seminary. Hodge was a conventional Presbyterian theologian. His tradition was one that valued common sense and which saw no demarcation between science and religion.[103] He was also a fallibilist with no illusions as to the absolute certainty of anything. This, coupled with his preparedness to engage in interdisciplinary debate may help model a way for us to consider the relationship between science and faith.

Hodge saw no reason to reject the science behind the theory of evolution. Darwin could be right in his science but wrong in his philosophy.[104] Hodge recognized that the key point was whether or not humankind was a product of chance or design. He saw that denial of design was tantamount to atheism and feared (correctly, as it happened) that Darwinism would be inflated into a naturalistic world-view that would rival or even counter religion.[105] Hodge therefore left open the possibility of an alternative interpretation of the Darwinian thesis which could include divine involvement and providence.[106]

What can be said in summary? Even accounting for the myths and exaggerations surrounding Darwin and Christianity, Darwinian thinking heralded a low point in science's relationship with theology that was to continue until recent times. As John Durrant says, "First in cosmology with Galileo, then in biology with Darwin, and finally in psychology with Freud, we are confronted with the fact that we are mere fragments in a world that appears to be neither about us nor for us."[107]

One of the added difficulties for faith caused by Darwin's theory of evolution was that it generated a philosophical momentum of its own that went well beyond the field of science. This, as the theologian Mark Worthing points out, made it difficult for Christian supporters of Darwin to separate his scientific theory from the philosophical Darwinism that was rapidly gaining ground in intellectual circles.[108] Darwinism became synonymous with emancipation from ignorance and religion. Its tenor was exemplified by John Draper who wrote in the final paragraph of his book, "Faith must render an account of herself to Reason. Mysteries must give place to facts. Religion must relinquish that . . . domineering position which she has so long maintained against science."[109]

TODAY: SCIENCE AND THEOLOGY IN DIALOGUE

Happily, the situation has changed in recent times and there has been a renewed international interest in the relationship between science and religion. The scientist and theologian John Polkinghorne suggests that this active phase of conversation between the two disciplines began with the publication of Ian Barbour's book *Issues in Science and Religion* in 1966.[110] This may be so, but the change in thinking that allowed this conversation was heralded earlier by people such as the Hungarian chemist Michael Polanyi (1890–1976) who, as we shall see later, helped free science from its empiricist prison, making it possible for the two disciplines to dialogue. The extent to which the relationship between the two disciplines has changed persuades Mark Worthing to say that there is little doubt that we are undergoing a paradigm shift of such significance that "a new era in the history of science and theology is being heralded."[111] This is evidenced in the creation of new centers of research,[112] academic chairs and lectureships. There has been a burgeoning of associations of scientists and theologians interested in each other's discipline. In

Australia, these include: The Institute for the Study of Christianity in an Age of Science (ISCAST); the university Science-Faith network, the Symposium on Science and Theology of the Australian Theological Forum and the Centre for Theology Science and Culture based at Flinders University in Adelaide.[113] As science pushes its frontiers of knowledge, it is beginning to bump up against ultimate questions and this has helped prompt a new dialogue between the disciplines.

It can be concluded that portrayals of the negative relationship between science and theology in history are often simplistic. The relationship between science and religion is not one that has grown increasingly apart but is one that has continually changed throughout history. This relationship is currently one which is witnessing a renewed level of dialogue and co-operation between the two disciplines.

2

Science Allows Faith

I realized science couldn't answer any of the really interesting questions so I turned to philosophy and have been searching for God ever since."

—A LINE SPOKEN BY CHANTLAS IN THE FILM RED PLANET,
(WARNER BROS. VILLAGE ROADSHOW PICTURES, 1999)

THE OXFORD BIOLOGIST RICHARD Dawkins wrote a book with the provocative title, *The God Delusion*. It made the New York Times best seller list for many weeks. Dawkins begins chapter two of his book by describing Yahweh, the God of the Old Testament as:

> Arguably the most unpleasant character in all fiction. Jealous and proud of it, a petty, unjust, unforgiving control freak, a vindictive, bloodthirsty ethnic cleanser, a misogynistic, homophobic, racist, infanticidal, genocidical, philocidal, pestilential, megalomaniacal, sadomasochistic, capriciously malevolent bully.[1]

Later in his book he says, "God almost certainly does not exist . . . However statistically improbable the entity you seek to explain by invoking a designer, the designer himself has got to be at least as improbable. God is the Ultimate Boeing 747."[2]

The "Boeing 747" reference alludes to a statement made by the English physicist and astronomer Fred Hoyle (1915–2001). Notwithstanding his atheistic convictions, Hoyle had said that the likelihood that chance alone might be responsible for making even the simplest of living cells was about the same as "a tornado sweeping through a junk-yard (assembling) a Boeing 747 from the materials therein."[3] In his attack on Christianity, Dawkins turns Hoyle's saying around and suggests that any concept of God is just as unlikely as Hoyle's tornado-built Boeing 747. Dawkins will not permit any mystery that points to the possibility of God, even if it comes from a fellow atheist.

Is Dawkins right? Has science shown that belief in God is scientifically unreasonable? Evidently, many think this is the case. The results of the South Australian questionnaire conducted amongst tertiary trained people show that 84 percent of non-church goers agreed with some aspects of the sentiment represented by the statement: "Science challenges the credibility of the Christian faith."[4] The fact that 84 percent of non-church goers believe, to some extent, that science damages the credibility of Christianity is a highly disturbing statistic that needs to be addressed by Christians. To do this, we need to examine the convictions of people like Richard Dawkins who have helped fuel the idea that science has provided alternative explanations for the nature of the world and has made belief in God obsolete.

Unfortunately, it is very easy for scientists with personal ideological convictions regarding faith to give the misleading impression that their atheistic convictions are the product of pure, unassailable, scientific fact. The general public are usually not aware when such scientists switch from strict scientific reportage to making atheistic "faith" statements. In reality, such metaphysical claims are more often the result of pre-existing ideologies than the result of an accurate and balanced overview of science.

A CALL FOR HUMILITY

For progress to be made in the science–theology debate, it will be necessary for both scientists and theologians to retain a sense of humility in their claims. The scientific community needs to avoid the overbearing, all-controlling stance it once accused the Christian church of adopting at the start of the Enlightenment. Physicist and theologian John Polkinghorne is one who believes that facile triumphalism (arrogant, overbearing exclusivism) is now more of a problem of the secular academy than the Christian Church.[5] The biologist John Puddefoot reminds us that the solutions presented in science and theology are both the result of "fumblings and gropings which are an essential part of any discovery."[6] As such, science should not pretend to have the entire monopoly on truth.

There are two reasons for this: first, as post-modern thinking has reminded us, science can never be entirely objective and innocent of its human context. Second: science cannot be isolated from other forms of knowing if a more complete understanding of the ultimate meaning of things is being sought. Both science and theology come from a synthesis of people's experience of reality. Both share in the quest for understanding and both are the product of human experience and culture. Arthur Peacocke, scientist and theologian, says, "The scientific and theological enterprises share alike the tools of groping humanity—our stock of words, ideas and images that have been handed down, tools that we refashion in our own way for our own times in the light of experiment and experience."[7]

Lack of humility leads to both religious and agnostic extremes, each of which helps fuel the other. Stephen Gould's comment that humankind is no more than "a fortuitous twig, budding but yesterday on an ancient and copious bush of (evolution)"[8] is a personal conviction stated by a scientist. It is not a scientific fact, for it belies the reasoning of other scientists, such as the renowned physicist and cosmologist Paul Davies, who says:

> I belong to the group of scientists who do not subscribe to a conventional religion but nevertheless deny that the universe is a purposeless accident. Through my scientific work I have come to believe more and more strongly that the universe is put together with an ingenuity so astonishing that I cannot accept it merely as a brute fact . . . I cannot believe that our existence in this universe is a mere quirk of fate, an accident of history, an incidental blip in the great cosmic drama. Our involvement is too intimate . . . We are truly meant to be here.[9]

The Scottish neuroscientist Donald MacKay makes the comment that it seems to be the anti-religious apologists of our time who are seeking illicit support in scientific data for their metaphysical beliefs (or unbeliefs).[10] The theoretical physicist Steven Weinberg concludes his book, The First Three Minutes, saying that it is, "farcical to think that human beings were anything more than an "outcome of a chain of accidents reaching back to the first three minutes" . . . (Earth) is just a tiny part of an overwhelmingly hostile universe . . . The more the universe seems comprehensible, the more it also seems pointless."[11]

However, the very same information persuades Freeman Dyson, research physicist at the Advanced Institute at Princeton, to say, "The more I examine the universe and study details of its architecture, the more evidence I find that the universe in some sense must have known that we were coming."[12] This leads Dyson to say, "Twentieth Century science provides a solid foundation for a philosophy of hope."[13]

The risk in claiming certainty for philosophic pronouncements based on a purely scientific perspective is that science can be wrong. What we know today is not all there is to know. Scientific knowledge is continually evolving. The Australian astronomer, Robert Hanbury Brown writes that although science has proved to be highly effective and fruitful, it still "reserves the right to be wrong and then, if necessary, to change its mind."[14]

Science can not only be imperfect in its understanding but is also limited, in what it can know. The medical scientist Peter Medawar believes that existential questions such as " why are we here?" and "how did everything begin?" cannot be answered by science. He says that, "A limit upon science is made very likely by the existence of questions that science cannot answer and that no conceivable advance of science would empower it to answer. It is not to science, therefore but to metaphysics, imaginative literature or religion that we must turn for answers to questions having to do with first and last things."[15]

However, this limitation in no way devalues the importance of science, which Medawar considers to be humanity's greatest achievement.

The astronomer John Barrow goes further and gives some technical reasons why there are limits to what we can know through science. He speaks of the mental limits of knowing and how the universe's very structure prevents us from answering the deepest questions about its beginning and its future.[16]

Wolfhart Pannenberg, the German theologian, has also expressed concern at the inflated claims of science saying that by declaring scientific inquiry to be independent of religion, scientists are effectively denying religion any claim on the reality of nature. He says that, "In the area of public discourse religious assertions were considered superfluous with regard to human knowledge of the natural world. This meant that religion does not make any difference to the scientific description of the reality of nature and the logical implication was that religion has no legitimate claim on reality."[17] Pannenberg makes the point that if God is creator of the universe, then it is not possible to understand fully or even appropriately the process of nature without reference to that God. He fully appreciates that our understanding of the reality of God should not be incompatible with our knowledge of natural processes. However, science should not claim exclusive competence regarding the explanation of nature. He says that "the so-called methodological atheism of modern science is far from pure innocence"[18] and goes on to suggest that the very possibility we can do science is predicated on "the unfailing faithfulness of the creator God to his creation."[19]

The Scottish theologian Thomas Torrance says that science has generated an immensely powerful and successful conceptual machinery which has generated a momentum of its own, but risks locking itself into an empiricist prison that cannot allow for the possibility of God's action. By continuing to deny the possibility of God's action, scientists risk shutting the door on a fuller appreciation of truth.[20] Torrance argues that the contingency (happen-stance) and order of the universe uncovered by science require a better explanation. Therefore, it is reasonable to contemplate the possibility of God.[21] There is, then, a need for moderation and humility in the claims of scientists.

Needless to say, theologians need to be equally honest and humble about the things of which they are convinced. Fruitful dialogue can only occur when both make room for the other. If we fail to be open to each other's discipline, truth is at risk. A salutary lesson in this is afforded by recounting the story of how the Big Bang theory came to be understood.

It is significant that both biblical literalists and atheistic scientists have opposed the Big Bang theory for ideological reasons rather than scientific ones. A reluctance to address scientific evidence is therefore not the exclusive preserve of biblical literalists. An example of this was the unwillingness of the English physicist, Fred Hoyle, to admit to the possibility of the big bang, despite mounting scientific evidence. The extent of this evidence is worth recounting.

In 1917, Einstein proposed a model for the universe based on the "cosmological principle." This stated that matter in the universe was both homogeneous (evenly distributed) and isotropic (having similar physical properties in every direction) when viewed on a very large scale. However, when Einstein applied the cosmological principle to his theory of general relativity, he discovered that the universe could not be static but must either be expanding or contracting. To solve the problem of why matter in the universe did not clump back together under the force of gravity, Einstein introduced a "cosmological constant," a theoretical repulsive force which he suggested must exist to balance the force of gravity and result in a static universe.[22] He was later to describe his belief in a static universe as the biggest mistake of his life.

Einstein's mistake was understandable given that telescopes had not yet established that the universe extended beyond the Milky Way. The velocities of stars that could be seen were so small that they indicated that the universe was spatially finite, of infinite age and static in size. The enormous spatial extent of the universe beyond our own galaxy was only firmly established in the early 1920s from observations made using the Mt. Wilson 100 inch telescope. As it turns out, Einstein may not have been quite as mistaken as he believed. Recent evidence has uncovered the possibility of the existence of dark energy which works in opposition to gravity. Astronomers looking at supernovas between six and eight billions years old, discovered that the rate of expansion of the universe had slowed down until approximately 6.3 billion years ago when it apparently speeded up and accelerated. This suggested the existence of another force which was able to take over once the gravitational forces holding the physical bodies in the universe together had largely dissipated due to the growing distances between cosmic bodies. This new force was therefore one that was able to affect the properties of the Universe over very large distances.[23] It has been estimated that dark energy comprises 73 percent of the mass-energy budget of the universe. The rest of the universe is thought to be made up of 4 percent visible matter and 23 percent dark matter. Although there is still some skepticism over the existence of dark energy, a standard model of cosmology has emerged and seems to be consistent with all observations. Ever since it was known the the universe was expanding, scientists have wondered whether the expansion would go on forever, or if common gravity might eventually win out and pull everything back together in a sort of Big Crunch. The probable existence of dark energy suggests the former as the likely scenario.

Einstein's idea of a static universe was challenged when the American astronomer Vesto Slipher noticed in 1917 that the spectral lines of distant large "spiral nebulae" were shifted toward the red wavelength. This could only be caused by the Doppler effect of the galaxies moving away from our own galaxy. In other words, our universe was expanding. A further challenge came in 1922, when a Russian mathematician, Alexander Friedman, discovered an error in Einstein's proof for a static universe and showed that an expanding or contracting universe was possible.[24] The fact that the universe was expanding was finally confirmed by observations by the American astronomer Edwin Hubble in 1929 who discovered that the more remote the galaxy, the faster it was moving away.[25]

In 1948, the Russian-American physicist George Gamow (with the help of the mathematics of his old tutor, the Russian scientist Alexander Friedmann) developed a theory put forward by the Belgian priest and cosmologist, Georges Lemaître in 1927. It was the idea that the universe exploded out from a highly compressed and extremely hot particle which he called the "primeval atom." Gamow presented what has come to be known as the Big Bang theory of the origin of the universe.[26] Gamow further predicted that if the residual radiation from such an explosion must still exist, it would now measure approximately minus 268°C.

In 1964, Arno Penzias and Robert Wilson of Bell Laboratories turned a large radio receiver towards space and discovered that no matter where they pointed it, they were getting a signal indicating the presence of microwaves. These proved to be Gamow's predicted residue from the Big Bang.[27] The COBE (Cosmic Background Explorer) satellite launched in 1989 to study this cosmic microwave background discovered that the residual Big Bang microwave had, in fact, now cooled to minus 270.3°C and had a spectrum which exactly matched that which was predicted.[28]

Further evidence was to follow two years later. Scientists (such as the Russian astrophysicist Yakov Zeldovich) reasoned that in order for galaxies to be formed, there would need to be slight ripples in the background radiation which represented slight variations in the uniformity of matter distributed in the universe. This was necessary to allow matter to clump together to form clusters of galaxies. In 1992, these density ripples in the microwave background were discovered by the same COBE space satellite.[29]

The reason for mentioning the sequence of discoveries in some detail is to make the point that evidence for the cosmic Big Bang is very compelling.[30] However, despite this, Hoyle, a committed atheist, did not want to consider anything so inexplicable as a beginning. Instead, he promoted the 1948 "steady state theory" of Bondi and Gold which suggested that the universe was expanding but kept producing matter as it expanded so that the density of heavenly bodies in the universe stayed the same. The universe could then be said to have always been. No God was necessary to switch it on.

Hoyle's promotion of the steady state theory initially had a basis to it. In 1950, the earth was thought to be over 4 billion years old, but the age of the universe, (estimated by its rate of expansion), was thought only to be 2 billion years old. Even though this puzzling discrepancy was resolved a few years later, Hoyle continued to hold to the steady state theory, and did so even after Penzias and Wilson identified the background radiation of the Big Bang. It is significant to note that his motive for holding out against this scientific evidence was not motivated by science but by his philosophic mind-set. Hoyle admitted, "The big bang theory requires a recent origin of the universe that openly invites the concept of creation."[31]

An example of a philosopher of the same period who allowed his scientific thinking to be constrained by atheism is Bertrand Russell. He felt we had to accept the existence of the universe simply as a brute fact. In a BBC debate he said, "the universe is just there, and that's all." He did not want to think about anything that might invite the possibility of God.[32]

It is perhaps significant that ideology also led Soviet cosmologists to be suspicious of, or to reject the idea of the Big Bang theory. McMullin mentions a book by V. I. Sviderskii published in 1956 which rejected the Big Bang model describing it as an "unscientific Popish conclusion."[33] V. A. Ambartsumian, another leading Soviet astrophysicist, declared in 1959 that the advances in science demonstrate the "unsoundness of . . . the religious world-view."[34] Whilst he now no longer asserts that defenders of the Big Bang model were motivated by a religious worldview, he continues to reject the model by saying that notions of the universe having an age contain so many assumptions as to be useless and, by this comment, he sweeps an unpalatable notion under the rug.

A mindset this closed to the possibility of God not only makes fruitful dialogue with theologians impossible but also threatens the credibility of science. We have to search for greater humility and honesty if mutually beneficial progress is to be made in our understanding of reality. It is perfectly reasonable to hold to an ideology but, in all fairness, it needs to be presented as a faith statement, not fact. For example, the vastness of the universe has helped persuade some non-Christian scientists of our insignificance. The biologist Jacques Monod has said, "The ancient covenant is in pieces: man at last knows that he is alone in the unfeeling immensity of the universe, out of which he has emerged only by chance. Neither his destiny nor his duty have been written down."[35]

This statement is presented as scientific fact notwithstanding the fact that other scientists, such as the physicist, Robert Russell, see the same universe and conclude that we must reflect on the serious possibility of God. He makes his point saying, "Suppose you are lost and thirsty in a vast, dry desert. Suddenly you spot a palm tree on the horizon. Are you going to say, 'Well since the desert is so vast and barren, that wavy tree is insignificant, a statistical fluke not worth taking seriously'"[36]

The glasses you wear will affect what you see

When the biologist Richard Dawkins makes the statement: "In a universe of blind physical forces and genetic replication, some people are going to get hurt, other people are going to get lucky, and you won't find any rhyme or reason in it, nor any justice,"[37] physicist and theologian John Polkinghorne suggests that it is not Dawkins' knowledge of genetics that causes him to make such a pronouncement so much as his metaphysical judgment[38] What Dawkins sees as meaningless, Polkinghorne understands as being the consequence of a world allowed by its Creator to make itself. Dawkins sees a meaningless world of genetic competition whilst Polkinghorne sees the reality of a world allowed by the Creator to explore its own inherent fruitfulness.[39] Neither position has been scientifically proven. The language of secular scientists therefore needs to be careful in its claims, particularly as non-scientists may not have the skill to determine when a scientist strays from empirical data to philosophical speculation.

Because Richard Dawkins is arguably the most articulate anti-Christian scientist today, it is worth examining his claims to see if it is valid to argue for consonance (mutually supportive harmony) between science and theology.[40] Dawkins argues that evolution works at the level of the gene. Genes occupy and then discard bodies. The survival of genes (specifically DNA) is, therefore, the true purpose of life.[41] This, of course, begs the question of how and why DNA became so clever. How did genetic codes gets encoded in DNA in the first place? These questions suggest that Dawkins may not have pointed to the ultimate causal agent of change so much as pointed to the tool the ultimate causal agent of change uses.

It is Dawkins' conviction that highly improbable complex end products of evolution can be accomplished with gradual stepwise changes. He says that, "Evolutionary high ground cannot be approached hastily. Even the most difficult problems can be solved, and even the most precipitous heights can be scaled, if only a slow, gradual, step-by-step pathway can be found."[42] Dawkins' language might suggest that an organism evolves towards a goal but this is not what he means. Evolution has no "goal." The organization of biological structures is the result of countless small steps of evolutionary change, each of which confer an improvement over a previous stage which helps an organism (or its DNA) to survive. There is, therefore, no evolutionary ladder with humans at the top. Evolution is a branching tree and "that's all there is to it."[43] According to Dawkins, questions of ultimate meaning such as, Who am I?, Why am I? and, What is the meaning to life?, simply reflect the fact that Homo sapiens is a deeply purpose-ridden species unable to come to terms with its meaninglessness.

Dawkins says, "This is a world where DNA neither cares nor knows. DNA just is. And we dance to its music."[44] Dawkins needs to be careful here. To simply say that DNA "just is" is an inadequate response to the highly unlikely, mind-boggling complexity of DNA. Similarly, to declare the human search for meaning to be meaningless is as much a faith statement as any found in religion. It is reasonable to suggest that the human ache for meaning deserves a better explanation.

We need also to ask why Dawkins' evolution has not only molded our bodies but also the philosophically mysterious workings of human consciousness. Dawkins concedes that the "mysterious crossing of the neuron threshold" is a profound mystery,[45] but is nonetheless confident that there will eventually be a rational evolutionary explanation for all human brain states.[46] The moral theologian, Keith Ward, does not share his optimism and says that this is a mystery that biology can never solve because it is not a biological mystery to begin with.[47]

Dawkins' neo-Darwinian position has been challenged by some scientists who support the concept of Intelligent Design. Intelligent Design is the resurfacing of William Paley's conviction that the complexity of living organisms points to the existence of a Creator. It claims that evolution alone cannot adequately explain the complexity we see in living organisms, a complexity that suggests intelligent design.

The concept of Intelligent Design will be discussed further in the final chapter. What we will discuss now is whether Intelligent Design represents a valid challenge to the thinking of Richard Dawkins.

As has been said, Dawkins claims that all complex biological systems are the product of a multitude of infinitesimal changes. This theory accounts well for change where each step of change confers an advantage over the previous step. However, it is sometimes difficult to envisage how any intermediate step could have conferred any advantage to a living organism. An example of the sort of change that is hard to explain is the development by the "bombardier beetle" (Stenaptinus insignis) of its unique form of defense This beetle secretes two chemicals into a chamber in its abdomen, hydroquinone and hydrogen peroxide. When the beetle is threatened by an attacker it squirts this chemical mix into another chamber which contains a catalytic enzyme which causes the two chemicals to react together violently and boil. The resultant hot noxious spray is then squirted accurately through two tubes in the end of its abdomen at any aggressor threatening the beetle. The biochemist Michael Behe[48] cites this as an example of "irreducible complexity," i.e., it is a system so complicated that it could not be something that could have been achieved incrementally by evolution. Too many parallel developments would need to happen for which it is difficult to imagine any benefit to the survival of any intermediate step.[49]

Appealing to the sophistication of the bombardier beetle as evidence of God's intelligent design may seem attractive, but it is dangerous, for we would then need to ask why God made the ichneumon wasp that was so abhorrent to Darwin, or why God designed the tape-worm or the candirus fish (Vandellia cirrhosa) of South America. This tiny, parasitic catfish can swim up the urinary tract of humans and embed itself into position with the backward facing spines around its head. Once in position, it feeds on the blood from the wound it makes. Understandably, it is extraordinarily difficult to remove.

The claim of "irreducible complexity" pointing to God's intentional design not only has philosophical difficulties but also scientific ones. The claims of "irreducible complexity" have been refuted by a number of reputable scientists.[50] Certainly, related beetles showing less sophisticated use of the same chemicals do exist in the beetle kingdom.[51] One therefore has to take seriously the possibility that evolution is able to result in very sophisticated life-forms and behaviors through incremental change. As Stephen Jay Gould says, "Every naturalist has his favorite example of awe-inspiring adaptation." His is the fish-like appendage found on some species of the freshwater genus of mussel Lampsilis which lies partly buried in the bottom of the lake. Riding atop the protruding end is a structure that looks for all the world like a little fish. It has a streamlined body, well-designed side flaps that undulate in a swimming motion, a tail and even an eye-spot. When a real fish comes to investigate it, the mussel discharges its larvae (glochidia) which find their way to the fish's gills which they parasitize. When they mature, they rupture the cysts they cause to grow on the fish's gills and fall to the lake floor where they complete their adult life.[52]

In view of the sophisticated life forms that can develop as a result of incremental change, the concept of Intelligent Design does not seriously challenge Dawkins' thinking, even though he is not always persuasive in giving adequate explanations for intermediate evolutionary steps, for example, when talking about the elaborate dance language of honey bees. Evidently, when food is found by a bee near the hive, it does a "round dance" which tells other bees that food is near the hive. However, when food is further away, the bee performs a "waggle dance" in the dark of a hive on the vertical surface of the comb. The waggle dance is performed in a figure of eight with a straight turn in the middle pointing to the direction of the food, relative to the sun. Other bees have learnt to feel the dance (they are unable to see it), and translate the vertical dance inside the hive to the horizontal reality outside. They also determine from the dance how far away the food is from the hive. Dawkins explains that this could all have evolved from a bee taking a longer take-off run to go back to the food source that it had found.[53]

Whilst Dawkins' lack of humility in presenting his case makes him vulnerable to criticism, it must be acknowledged that the evolutionary theory has proved to be an excellent, well attested model that explains the development of the diversity of life forms that exist. The Oxford chemist and theologian, Arthur Peacocke, states unequivocally that no professional, informed biologist works honestly without acknowledging the correctness of evolutionary theory. However, he goes on to say that evolution does not fully lift the veil on the mystery surrounding the existence of created life and lists twelve eminent biologists who believe that evolution does not yet adequately explain how distinctly new species come about.[54] Dawkins' theories do not explain why this universe is so inherently fruitful or why human consciousness seeks answers to ultimate questions. The evolutionary development of human consciousness, to the extent that it is able to ask the ultimate questions, is significant. Whilst one can understand how intelligence naturally arises through evolutionary processes because it confers a significant advantage when it comes to survival, the same can not so easily be said for our sense of the transcendent. Is the ability to ask ultimate questions simply a factor of intelligence or is it more significant? Certainly, there does seem to be a sense of incompleteness with the purely temporal world which St Augustine voiced well when he said, "thou hast made us for thyself and restless is our heart until it comes to rest in thee."[55]

It is important for scientists to be humble in their claims and to know the boundaries they can speak about with authority. If this constraint is ignored, truth may become the first casualty for it will be be shown in chapter 3 that far from science making faith obsolete, scientific discoveries have revealed a universe that seems remarkably suited to the development of life, a fact that has compelled many scientists to acknowledge that theistic faith is reasonable.

EVOLUTION OR ADAPTATION?

Some have suggested that whilst they can accept that an organism can change to adapt to different environments, they don't really evolve into new species.

The short answer to this is that they can, but first, it might be helpful to define what the process of evolution is. Evolution is a genetic change in an individual selected by nature to thrive because it helps the individual thrive in a particular ecological niche. As a general rule, taxonomists (who name and categorize living organisms) declare that an organism has evolved into a new species when it has changed so much that it can no longer mate with its original parent species.

Numerous accounts of speciation (the development of new species) exist. Seven discreet populations of the Larus spp (herring gull and black-backed gull) are found around the edge of the Arctic. It is thought that populations of the Larus spp changed as they migrated around the edge of the Arctic until the resultant species had changed so much they could no longer mate with the original parent species.

The generation of new species can be particular rapid in plants, largely because of the habit they occasionally have of doubling their chromosomes (an event called 'polyploidy') which results in new species being formed.

The process of evolution is therefore observable and measurable.

THEOLOGICAL HUMILITY

Whilst it is important for science to allow for faith, the reciprocal is also true. The importance of theological humility in the face of science must also be acknowledged.

It is not my intention to dwell on the more extreme views of biblical literalists such as T. LaHaye, D. A. Noebel, C. Matrisciana, and R. Oakland other than to note that they see conventional science being controlled by evil which seeks to suppress true, Godly science. They see Godly science as being consistent with a literalist understanding of Scripture. Much of what is presented as conventional science is therefore seen as a conspiracy against God, designed to deceive humankind and keep them from honoring God's word in Scripture and thereby encountering God.[56]

Not surprisingly, the views of such authors lack credibility to most scientists of repute, some of whom have written savage critiques of such literalist understandings.[57] Therefore, in the interests of both truth and fruitful dialogue, apologists should distance themselves from such a literalist understanding for it will rightly fuel the incredulity and contempt of the scientific community. Christians need to be humble enough to accept that conventional scientists can uncover for us how the universe works. This truth is part of the general knowledge God has made available to all in the hope that everyone would wonder at, if not the majesty of God, certainly the possibility of God (Psalm 19:1–4; Romans 1:20).

There is also the need for humility in the claims made by Christians who are not Biblical literalists. An example of the need for this is illustrated by examining the conviction of Keith Ward, that the evolution of human consciousness from a state where no values are apprehended to a state where values exist, is highly significant. This persuades him that religious belief in a guiding creative force is reasonable.[58] Ward is on dangerous ground here as he comes close to suggesting that science cannot fully explain human thinking and therefore we need to postulate a God who makes it possible. In saying this, he seems to adopt the discredited "God of the gaps" theory which attributes to the hand of God gaps in knowledge that science cannot yet explain. This sort of understanding simply leads to continual theological retreat in the face of progressing scientific knowledge. However, there is a dilemma. Whilst Christians must not simply seek recourse to the "God of the gaps," the whole basis of natural theology is the claim that it is possible to see the hand of God in the creation and maintenance of the universe.

Scientists are rightly protective of their scientific method which has looked for natural, measurable causes for things which might otherwise lazily be attributed to God.[59] Their investigations have resulted in much fruitful understanding. Agnostic or atheist scientists will therefore hold very real fears for the integrity of science if the possibility of God is allowed, unless theology is modest in its claims.

HOW ARE WE TO UNDERSTAND THE CREATION ACCOUNTS IN GENESIS?[60]

Any call for theological humility would be deficient if it did not touch on the subject of how Christians should understand the biblical creation accounts in the first two chapters of Genesis.

A number theories have been advanced as to how these creation accounts should be understood. Some seem quite contrived and fanciful, others require a denial of scientific evidence. What all of them indicate is that it is not easy to resolve what sort of literature the opening chapters of Genesis are. As such, a degree of theological humility is appropriate. Some of the main theories that have been advanced include:

1) GENESIS IS A SCIENTIFIC TEXT BOOK

This is largely a nineteenth century understanding. It was promulgated in the twentieth century by the American young-earth creationist, Henry M. Morris (1918–2006). Young earth creationists takes seriously the work of Bishop James Usher (1581–1656), Archbishop of Armagh, who examined biblical records of genealogies and concluded that the earth must have been created in 4004 BC.

In order for Henry Morris to believe the earth was only a bit over 6,000 years old, he believed that God had made the earth with a partial appearance of age. Despite believing this, he firmly discounted the significance of fossil records and any idea that biological diversification came through the agency of evolution.

Morris backed his claims by suggesting that the speed of light had changed through history. However, it was found that the error bars (that gave the confidence limits to his calculations) were so huge that there was, in reality, no evidence for any change in the speed of light at all.

It is also worth noting that in order to support the evidence for a young earth, some have claimed that human footsteps were found together with dinosaur footprints in the petrified mud of Paluxy River in Texas.[61] However, a closer inspection that the allegedly human footprints showed them to be either depressions of weathered rock or the footprints of small dinosaurs. Eventually, John D. Morris, (son of

Henry Morris), head of the Institute for Creation Research, reported in the January 1986 issue of his publication Impact that "it would now be improper for creationists to continue to use the Paluxy data as evidence against evolution."

2) God made the universe old (with perfect 'antiquing')

This idea was promoted by the English naturalist, Phillip Gosse (1810–1888). The problem with this theory is: why would God do this? Why would God hide fossils in geological formations and make Adam with a navel? Such an idea rather suggests God is a deceiver.

3) The Gap theory

This theory was promoted by Thomas Chalmers (1780–1847), a Scottish theologian. He suggested there was huge gap of indeterminate time between the first two verses of the Bible. This gap in time was caused by the fall of Satan which caused the earth God created to become formless and empty. God then needed to reconstruct the universe (a process called 'ruin reconstruction') to be what it is today. This theory therefore allows for the existence of dinosaur fossils, as these are seen as the remains of the previous ruined universe.

4) Days are really 'ages'

This theory was promoted by Hugh Miller (1802–1856) a Scottish geologist and theologian. He suggested that when Genesis uses the term 'day' it really means a huge span of time. Those who hold to this theory cite Psalm 90:4 and 2 Peter 3:8 where a day is equated to a thousand years.

> But do not forget this one thing, dear friends: With the Lord a day is like a thousand years, and a thousand years are like a day.
> (2 Pet 3:8)

It needs to be said, however, that this passage was written to teach that God is not constrained by time. It was not designed to teach that God's year equals one thousand human years.

5) The days of creation are really days of revelation

The best known exponent of this theory was Air-Commodore P. J. Wiseman (an Assyriologist) who set out his ideas in his book *Creation Revealed in Six Days*. He believed that days of creation were not really days of creation but days of revelation. This understanding relies on an imaginative rewriting of the first verse of the Bible so that it reads: "In the beginning, God made <u>known</u> the heavens and the earth."

6) Genesis is a tapestry of many literary forms

This understanding results from a careful examination of the question: what sort of literature are the first twelve chapters of Genesis? It is not easy to answer this question as the style of writing in Genesis has few parallels. We don't instinctively interpret it as poetry, history or science. So, what is it?

The theologian and astrophysicists, Dr David Wilkinson, (currently Principal of St. John's College, Durham University) suggests that Genesis is a tapestry of many styles of writing:

- It has poetical elements such as the repeated phrases, 'and it was so' and 'it was good." Some also see significance in the number of times key words are repeated. There is certainly a pattern. Three days of forming the universe are followed by three days of filling it.
- It contains theological principles that teach 'who' and 'why' rather than scientific principles of 'how' and 'when.'
- It is a hymn of worship.
- It contains some history (from chapter 12 onwards).

By suggesting that Genesis is a tapestry made up of all these threads, no one literary form has to be insisted on. As such, Genesis is rescued from having a literalistic straight-jacket imposed on it, a constriction that the original writers never intended.

Ever since the Christian church was quite young, the leaders of the church have come to understand that the first two chapters of Genesis (which speak about God creating the universe) were written to answer the theological questions of who and why rather than science's questions of how and when. These chapters teach the fundamental principles upon which the rest of the Bible is based. With peerless prose, they declare:

1. in an age of polytheism, that there is only one God
2. in an age when people try to worship creation, that all creation is created by God

3. in an age when the gods were thought not to care, that God thought his creation was fantastic and that he seeks a loving relationship with us.
4. in an age which fails to explain the reality of evil, that evil is rebellion against God.
5. in an age that cannot make sense of suffering, that suffering is the result of humankind going down a path God never intended.
6. in an age that feels helpless in the jaws of suffering,—God has not given up on us.
7. in an age that despairs of finding justice and which tolerates evil, God declares that he has a zero tolerance to evil and that he will ensure that justice will ultimately prevail.
8. in an age that has lost God amongst its religions and philosophies, God is rescuing his people and his creation back to himself.

Good theology that takes into account the context and literary form of Scripture will prevent Christians from engaging in ill-founded biblical literalism. It will also result in a more humble, non-adversarial attitude to science because it understands that scientific truth is a universally valid truth which exists independently of religious dogma. Theological humility is also required if all of life's mysteries are not to be triumphantly attributed to God, for scientists are rightly scornful of anything that smacks of the "God of the gaps."

The proper role of theology is not to oppose science but to set science in a deeper context. As John Polkinghorne says, theology asks if "there is more to be understood about these (laws of nature) beyond mere assertion."[62] As such, it seeks to complement science, going beyond its realm of inquiry to address the big questions, such as why things are as they are and why are the workings of the universe intelligible to us?

HOW CAN SCIENCE AND THEOLOGY RELATE?

How should the disciplines of science and faith relate? In his book *Religion in an Age of Science* the scientist and theologian Ian Barbour lists four possible ways that science can relate to religion.[63] His categories are:

1) Conflict

Those who advocate conflict between the disciplines of science and theology include the scientists Richard Dawkins, Francis Crick, Carl Sagan, and Peter Atkins.

2) Independence

Total independence between the disciplines of science and theology is proposed by the theologian Karl Barth and the biologist Simon Gould.[64] Both say that the two disciplines of science and theology are distinctive disciplines that have no relation to each other and that any dialogue will make presumptions that are dangerous.

3) Dialogue

Dialogue between science and faith is advocated by Ian Barbour, Alister McGrath, Arthur Peacocke, Ted Peters, John Polkinghorne, Thomas Torrance, and Mark Worthing.

4) Integration

Integration seeks to make a theology of science. This has been proposed by the Jesuit anthropologist Pierre Teilhard de Chardin,[65] James Lovelock,[66] and the panentheists Charles Hartshorne,[67] John Cobb,[68] and Charles Birch.[69]

As a scientist and theologian who advocates dialogue, Arthur Peacocke welcomes the new perspectives afforded by the natural sciences. He believes this will not only provide a new context for the debate about how God acts but will also "give new conceptual resources for modeling it."[70] John Polkinghorne, another scientist and theologian, believes that dialogue between science and theology can be fruitful and that their relationship with each other should be one of consonance. Consonance means that science and theology should be in harmony with each other and not contradict each other. As such, some limited interplay between the two disciplines is possible. This allows science to contribute to theology for it recognizes that whilst science does not determine theological thought, it certainly constrains it. Polkinghorne is, however, nervous of complete assimilation of the two disciplines as he feels that assimilation will always carry the risk of theology being overwhelmed by science so that it is unheard.[71]

Not all theologians accept Barbour's fourfold summary of how science and faith relate. Holmes Rolston believes that it is too generic. He argues for a more nuanced approach that would allow for better dialogue between some disciplines than others. This would encourage theological dialogue with physics and cosmology (disciplines that seem more open to dialogue with theology) whilst recognizing that such dialogue may not be as fruitful with biologists who seem less inclined to dialogue with theologians.[72] His point that some scientific disciplines seem more open to theological dialogue than others is, perhaps, important to understand.

Ted Peters gives a more comprehensive list of the alternative ways science can relate to theology. He lists eight alternatives that currently exist:[73]

1) SCIENTISM

Scientism seeks war with religion in order to destroy it and win a total victory for science. Fred Hoyle and his personal view that religious behavior is an escapist measure pursued by people who seek illusory security in face of the mysteries of the universe,[74] would be one that Peters puts in this category, along with Stephen Hawking, Carl Sagan, and Francis Crick. Richard Dawkins would also fit here.

2) SCIENTIFIC IMPERIALISM

Scientific imperialists see science as a surer path to God than religion. Peters puts Paul Davies and Frank Tipler in this category.

3) ECCLESIAL AUTHORITARIANISM

This view believes that science must submit to ecclesial dogma.

4) SCIENTIFIC CREATIONISM

Scientific creationism believes that Biblical truth (understood in a literal way) and scientific truth are the same. Where there is conflict, science is inadequately understood.

5) THE TWO LANGUAGE THEORY

This recognizes that science and theology speak two different languages. Science asks 'how,' religion asks 'why.' A person can belong to both camps as their disciplines are quite different. This approach, popularized by the theologian Langdon Gilkey, seeks to gain peace by separation.

Timothy Ferris is also one who says that it is important not to overstate the convergence of science and religion and says "Good walls make good neighbors"[75] However, Werner Heisenberg (famous for his work in quantum theory) is not persuaded by this option saying, "I doubt whether human societies can live with so sharp a distinction between knowledge and faith."[76]

6) Hypothetical consonance

This approach has been promoted by Ernan McMullin who believes there is some accord between the truth of theologians and scientists. Both have common questions about transcendent reality.

7) Ethical overlap

Those who believe in ethical overlap believe that both disciplines should work together on ethical issues such as the environment. (It is possible to hold to this conviction as well as to belong to one of the other groups.)

8) New Age spirituality

This seeks a holistic approach, combining science with a wide range of spiritualities.

Of all the options mentioned, the seeking of consonance between the two disciplines would seem to be the most reasonable. Both disciplines are, as suggested by Polkinghorne, intellectual cousins under the skin for both are searching for motivated belief. "Neither can claim absolutely certain knowledge, for each must base its conclusions on an interplay between interpretation and experience."[77] Furthermore, they cannot be confined to their separate compartments and ignore each other. Fraser Watts, lecturer in Theology and the Natural Sciences at the University of Cambridge, agrees. He says, "They are each concerned with truth and there cannot be multiple truths which are completely unconnected with each other."[78]

Choosing to allow consonance between the disciplines of science and theology expresses the conviction that the two disciplines have something to say to each other. This view was expressed by Pope John Paul II, who wrote, "Science can purify religion from error and superstition: religion can purify science from idolatry and false absolutes. Each can draw the other into a wider world, a world in which both can flourish."[79]

Einstein echoed this sentiment in one of his famous aphorisms, "Science without religion is lame, religion without science is blind."[80]

What is it that the two disciplines can say to each other? Science can help constrain theologians so that they avoid theological excesses and pull back from ungrounded speculation. Polkinghorne says:

> What science can do for theology is to tell it what the physical world is actually like. In so doing, it imposes conditions of consonance which the broader considerations of theology must respect . . . The need for consonance with the findings of science can be a healthy corrective for theology, whose persistent temptation is to indulge in ungrounded speculation.[81]

In a later book, Polkinghorne goes on to explain what religion can do for science: He says, "Religion can offer science a deeper and more comprehensive account of reality within which the latter's search for understanding can find an intellectually comfortable home."[82] Without theology, science will struggle to make sense of why things are as they are. Without theology, science can seek to dissolve the mystery of the universe's existence by seeking lazy recourse to a grab-bag of "infinites" (that make anything possible) and passing this off as scientific fact. Science and theology are different disciplines with different languages but they must be allowed to speak to each other. Both disciplines show aspects of truth and, if God exists, both disciplines must meet at the point of ultimate truth—God.

John Polkinghorne supports this view by making the point that science alone presents an incomplete and impoverished view of reality. He says that music would just be vibrations in the air and a beautiful painting would just be daubs of paint of known chemical composition. As part of its technique of inquiry, science ignores questions of value, but this does not mean that values do not exist.[83] Derek Burke, a biotechnologist and former Vice Chancellor of the University of East Anglia, takes much the same position. He reflects on the sterility of a purely mechanistic understanding of life and asks, "is there really so little to life? . . . Is there nothing (apart from science) that men and women down the ages have learnt that is worth retaining? And as for music, art, literature, aesthetics, they seem to have no place."[84]

Another area in which science alone fails to give adequate explanation, is the origin of our sense of morality. Polkinghorne does not believe that this sense of morality is adequately explained by genetic imprinting or tacit communal cultural agreement. He asks, "Did Oskar Schindler take great risks to rescue more than one thousand Jews from extermination because of some implicit calculation of genetic advantage?"[85] This leads Polkinghorne to say that science, our sense of moral duty, our aesthetic delight and our religious experience are all carriers of value and meaning– and that theism is able to tie this all together. Our moral intuitions are "intimations of the perfect divine will, our aesthetic pleasures a sharing of the Creator's joy, and our religious intuitions are whispers of God's presence."[86] Theism, he says, "is concerned with making total sense of the world."[87] It alone presents an adequately rich basis for understanding the world in that it readily accommodates the many layered character of a reality shot through with value. It "explains more, and is more intellectually satisfying."[88] As such, it must be taken seriously and be allowed a voice.

THE POSTMODERN 'WILD-CHILD'

It is worth asking before concluding this chapter whether scientific humility can be pushed so far that we dare not claim anything to be true at all. The apologist needs to understand that any dialogue between science and faith will take place within today's post-modern social context which has a tendency to eschew absolute truth in favor of relative truth. To what extent are we to hold to post-modernism's conviction that truth is relative?

Post-modern thinking about science speaks of constructivism which states that knowledge is not passively received information about independently existing structures but is something that is actively built up by a person. We do not find truth so much as construct viable explanations of our experiences.[89] As such, what are referred to as the laws of nature are merely the results of human construction. Nature may not have laws. Ernst von Glasersfeld (Emeritus Professor of Psychology at the University of Georgia) says, "The fact that scientific knowledge enables us to cope does not justify the belief that scientific knowledge provides a picture of the world that corresponds to an absolute reality."[90]

Constructivists do not, necessarily, deny reality. Most are realists who acknowledge that the universe, although unknowable, does actually exist apart from them thinking about it. Their conviction is rather that science is no more than the pursuit of useful models that we construct to help us make sense of reality, a reality that may in fact be a great deal more than science defines.

The alternative to constructivism is "critical realism." Critical realism, a term popularized by a number of people including John Polkinghorne,[91] Ian Barbour, Arthur Peacocke, and Wentzel van Huyssteen,[92] recognizes that what we can know is a reliable guide to what is the case, or as Polkinghorne is fond of saying, "epistemology models ontology"[93] (It was rumored he used to wear this phrase on a T-shirt around Cambridge. Perhaps only in a place like Cambridge could he get away with it!) Critical realists are committed to a realist point of view. They are convinced that scientific theories, although constrained by models and metaphors, represent the real world. As a critical realist, Polkinghorne acknowledges that knowledge, is to a degree, partial, revisable and mediated by the culture of our time but he believes this does not mean we should deny the truth of science. The alternative is to be lost in a "Kantian fog" in which appearance has no basis in reality.[94] This is why, as Polkinghorne says, most scientists consciously or unconsciously attempt to maximize the correlation between how we know things and how things really are in their essential nature. Justification for this comes from the fruitful success of such a strategy.[95] Reality cannot simply be what we believe it to be, because our cognitive faculties must be accurate enough in their representations of reality to enable us to survive. In other words, our sense of reality did not come from a vacuum but was forged against the experience of what worked.

Despite this, Nancy Murphy, Professor of Christian Philosophy at Fuller Theological Seminary, argues that we should avoid critical realism in favor of a more post-modern approach.[96] The point at issue is the extent to which we understand science to be constrained by our culture and human idiosyncrasies. Certainly, it needs to be recognized that fallible and subjective human elements are always present in science. Even Stephen Hawking says that any scientific account of the universe must be treated as a partial, provisional and revisable cosmology.[97] The difficulty is in determining the extent to which this is the case. Timothy Ferris is one who believes that humankind's fallibility in understanding science should not be overstated. Whilst he understands that science is progressive and cumulative (with new theories becoming refinements of older ones) he nonetheless asserts that there has been no major refuting of a well accepted scientific theory in the last one hundred years.[98]

To what extent can science be described as objective and religion subjective? Ian Barbour says that since the 1950s these sharp contrasts have been increasingly called into question. Science, it appears, is not as objective nor religion as subjective as has been claimed.[99] Even John Polkinghorne, criticized by the likes of Nancy Murphy for his critical realism, appreciates that there is a middle way of knowing between certainty and relativism.[100] He speaks of the Hungarian chemist and philosopher Michael Polanyi who advocated "a frame of mind in which I hold firmly to what I believe to be true, even though I know it might conceivably be false."[101] Polanyi believed that all knowledge was personal in nature and must involve personal commitment.

Polanyi had two understandings which may help us distill a right attitude to scientific knowledge. Firstly, he believed that there is a harmony of method over the whole range of knowledge (including science and theology). Secondly, he understood that assessment of evidence is always an act of discretionary personal judgment, and as such, must always be open to the possibility of correction. Science commits to rationality, not impersonal detachment.[102]

Polanyi's understanding encourages two things. First, it encourages science to be modest in claiming objectivity. Second, it factors in the human element when putting forward any truth claim. The English philosopher Stephen Toulmin reminds us that science is a context-oriented language. Whenever scientific concepts are divorced from the original context or overextended to answer questions it was never meant to answer, a mythology arises which science cannot be expected to underwrite. In order to combat these distorting mythologies, Toulmin suggests that science must recognize the human element and understand how this impinges on the doing of science.[103]

The South African theologian Wentzel van Huyssteen (who held the position of Professor of Theology and Science at Princeton Theological Seminary) gives some credence to post-modern thinking in the doing of science. He says that post-modern philosophy insists on respect for the local context of inquiry and should therefore resist any global interpretation of science that could constrain local inquiry.[104] Van Huyssteen's comment should not be taken as meaning that Newton's laws of gravity may be true in one locality but not in another, rather, that ways of interpreting data should not be restricted, for example, to a western, rational, empiricist view.

The book, The Academic Left and its Quarrels with Science, by Paul Gross and Norman Levitt was one of the first to explore the intellectual struggle between post-modernism and traditional scientific understanding. Gross and Levitt acknowledge that science is a cultural construct in the sense that the kind of science actually carried out tends to reflect economic interests and beliefs of society. However, they reject the idea that science does not report the 'real' world but is simply a discourse making statements that are valid only for a given community. Gross and Levitt argue, like Polkinghorne, that the world exists independently of our perspectives, prejudices, ideologies and languages, and that its workings are best understood by the discipline of science. They write, "The attempts to read scientific knowledge as the mere transcription of Western, male, capitalist social perspectives, or as the deformed handicraft of the prison-house of language, are hopelessly naive and reductionistic. They take no account of the specific logic of the sciences."[105]

Gross and Levitt's book did not arouse much interest amongst scientists as most of them simply ignore post-modernism. Justification for this was encouraged in 1996 when Alan Sokal, a physicist at New York University, published an essay in Social Text, entitled "Transgressing the Boundaries: Toward a Transformative Hermeneutic of Quantum Gravity."[106] The paper was a hoax, nonsense from start to finish, but was nonetheless published. Sokal revealed the hoax in another journal, Lingua Franca, which was published at the same time.[107] For many scientists, this simply confirmed the lack of credibility of those mounting a post-modern challenge to scientific thinking.

Whilst most scientists reject that fact that science is simply a social construct,[108] science has nonetheless benefited from today's post-modern climate in that it has helped dispel the illusion that its discipline is unsullied by the human context. It has also allowed mystery to crack open science's self-imposed empiricist prison. However, the breaking open of science has come at a price. Post-modernism has opened the Pandora's box of pluralism so that science has not so much been freed to dance with Christianity, but to dance with a myriad of dancing partners, many of which dance to different tunes. Can truth emerge from such chaos? Wentzel van Huyssteen says that Christian theology is suffering from a type of schizophrenia.[109] Whilst it makes use of the post-modern mindset in order to encourage people to explore other ways of knowing, it also tries to deny the post-modern freedom that allows the validity of every type of subjective religious experience. Van Huyssteen goes on to say that modernism's rejection of religion (that is seen as irrational) and post-modernism's pluralizing of religion (so that it allows anything) have both hindered profitable dialogue between science and theology.[110] It logically follows that progress is more likely to be made if the extremes of both modernist empiricism and post-modernist pluralism are avoided.

In summary, whilst recognizing the excesses and dangers of post-modernist thinking, post-modernism does encourage modesty in scientific claims by pointing out the personal and cultural context of truth claims. It also allows us to appreciate that mystery still exists. This understanding helps break science free of its empirical straight-jacket and allow for the fact that rationality can never be adequately housed within science alone.[111] Van Huyssteen says that room is therefore made for theology and science to "share deeply in the quest for a more comprehensive and interrelated knowledge of the origin, meaning and destiny of our universe."[112] If we neglect either discipline, we ignore a door into understanding reality in all its fullness. The neuroscientist Donald MacKay says, "Man's truest dignity can be realized only by facing up to reality, whatever the cost: whether it be at the cost of his self-esteem or anything else. If we predefine what that reality must be, in a spirit of self-sufficiency and proud rejection of any claims on our obedience by our Creator, we can block ourselves off from the one way in which we would discover what reality is about by coming to know its Giver."[113]

The change in thinking that has allowed disciplines such as theology to input into science has been given added momentum by scientific discoveries made in the last eighty years. These discoveries have challenged the old "deterministic" view that for every event in the physical world, there exists at least one prior event which causes it.[114] Things are not that simple any more. The discovery of Heisenberg's uncertainty principle[115] and the fact that sub atomic particles can appear and disappear at random in the quantum world means that there is now more mystery. As a result, science has become more amenable to philosophy and theology. This has helped spawn what has come to be known as "new physics"[116] which understands that belief in God is reasonable and, as such, is open to dialogue with philosophers and theologians. Francis Collins, who was Director of the Human Genome

Project concurs. He says, "There is a wonderful harmony in the complementary truths of science and faith"[117]

Science does not have the exclusive franchise on truth. It is therefore both reasonable and profitable to encourage consonance between the disciplines of science and theology. Both share deeply in the quest for understanding the origins and workings of our universe. We need both disciplines to understand the reality we experience. We need both to fully appreciate the hand of God.

3

Cosmic Order as Evidence for God

The heavens declare the glory of God;
the skies proclaim the work of his hands.
Day after day they pour forth speech:
night after night they display knowledge.
There is no speech or language
where their voice is not heard.
Their voice goes out into all the earth,
their words to the end of the world.

—Psalm 19:1-4

Paul Dirac (1902–1984), one of the founding fathers of quantum theory, spent his life looking for beautiful equations. He made an extraordinary assertion, saying that it was more important that there be beauty in scientific equations than that they should be right because if they were ugly, there was little chance they could be right. He said, "It is more important to have beauty in one's equations than to have them fit experiment. It seems that if one is working from the point of view of getting beauty in one's equations, and if one has a really good insight, one is on a sure line of progress."[1] Scientists have long wondered why the universe is so ordered and why it displays such extraordinary mathematical beauty. Could these features point to the possibility of God?

People seem to be divided over whether it does. The results of the South Australian questionnaire show that 48 percent of non church goers disagreed with the statement: "The order of the universe suggests the existence and purpose of God."[2] This means that over fifty percent could at least go part way to believing it. As such, the issue of God's apparent hand in directing the order of creation might be a good initial point of contact for Christians when talking to non-church goers about faith. However, the fact remains that nearly half of respondents indicated they had some difficulties with the idea that the order seen in creation indicates the existence of God. Is there cosmological evidence for the existence of God? What can science say to theologians? The Anthropic Principle

In the last few decades, a new natural theology has been embraced by some Christian scientists such as John Polkinghorne, Ian Barbour, and Arthur Peacocke. It is not the old style natural theology of Aquinas that talked of evidence for the existence of God. Nor is it the natural theology of William Paley who believed that the design of individual organisms was evidence of God's existence. Rather, it is based on the more modest observation that the universe exists in a very precise way that has allowed the development of complex living organisms including human beings.

Ours is the "baby-bear" universe

This phenomenon has come to be known as the "anthropic principle." The anthropic principle (anthropic, meaning "of humankind") was a term first introduced by Australian born Cambridge astrophysicist Brandon

Carter in a paper presented in Krakow, Poland in 1973 at a symposium held in commemoration of the 500th birthday of Copernicus.[3] His argument began with a discussion of Copernicus, whose heliocentric system (planets revolving around the sun) is often thought to have removed humankind from any privileged position in the universe. Carter, however, insisted that humankind is privileged in that we exist to observe it. If the universe had differed significantly in its size, age and character then intelligent life would not now be present to observe it. For example, if the strength of the gravitational force differed by just one one thousandth of its current value, all stars would be either blue giants or red dwarfs[4] With no stars like our sun available to nourish life, the universe would be without observers. However, the fact that it does have observers means that the nuclear, gravitational and electromagnetic forces have all fallen within the very narrow limits necessary to allow such observers to develop. Carter says, "What we can expect to observe must be restricted by the conditions necessary for our presence as observers."[5]

There are two main versions of the anthropic principle, the "weak" and the "strong" version.[6] The "weak" anthropic principle says that the universe contains properties compatible with the existence of an observer because, if it did not, no one would be here to observe it. We never could expect to observe a universe that is significantly different from our own because our existence depends on the prior existence of just such a universe.[7] This means that when considering how the universe might be different, scientists need to consider the odds, not against an infinity of all other possibilities (something that is referred to as the cosmological principle) but only against those that permit the emergence of life, life that is capable of observing the universe.

The "strong" anthropic principle differs in that it says that the universe exists as it does in order to allow the creation of observers within it. The universe was designed for life.[8] The strong version of the anthropic principle is more controversial because it suggests that there is a designed purpose between the structure of the universe and the existence of human beings. The incredible coincidences, including the need for the cosmic expansion rate to be fine tuned to better than one part in 1060 in order to generate a flat universe so that normal Euclidean geometry[9] could develop and life exist. Such coincidences have persuaded many that the universe is goal directed.

In the scientific community, it is the weak anthropic principle that enjoys particular credence.[10] Most scientists who embrace the idea of the anthropic principle think in terms of order rather than something that was specifically designed to allow life. However, John Polkinghorne is not impressed by the weak version of the anthropic principle for he believes that it fails to acknowledge the remarkable specificity of a world containing humankind. He says, "It amounts to no more than saying 'We're here because we're here,'" which, he says is "an intellectually lazy response to an unexpectedly precise requirement."[11] This is perhaps slightly unfair. It does say a little more than Polkinghorne asserts, for the weak version suggests that humankind exists because of very particular features of the universe.

It is evident that these "particular features" need to be extraordinarily precise if life, as we know it, is to develop in our universe. Polkinghorne describes our universe as being very special, "one in a trillion you might say."[12] Billions of things had to be just right if life, as we know it, was to evolve. After the initial big bang, the universe could not expand too quickly, otherwise it would become too dilute for anything to happen. On the other hand, if it expanded too slowly, gravity would have caused it to clump back together too quickly to allow anything to evolve. In fact, if the force of the big bang had differed by as much as 10–60 of its present value, (that is 1 followed by 60 zeros!) life could not have developed in the universe. Stephen Hawking puts it this way: "If the rate of expansion one second after the big bang had been smaller by even one part in a hundred thousand million million, the universe would have re-collapsed before it even reached its present size."[13]

The universe would also need to have matter scattered evenly throughout it, otherwise there would be catastrophically destructive cosmic turbulence. However, the distribution of matter could not be too even but have slight concentrations of matter in order to allow galaxies to form.

The nuclear forces that exist in the universe also had to be just right. If they had been even slightly weaker, we would have only hydrogen in the universe. If they were slightly stronger, only helium. As it was, the nuclear forces were just right to allow stable stars to develop the carbon and water necessary to develop life.[14] There needed to be a delicate balance between gravity and electromagnetism to allow these stars to burn uniformly for long periods of time at the right temperature to convert hydrogen and helium into carbon. Polkinghorne says, "Every atom of carbon inside our bodies was once inside a star. We are all made from the ashes of dead stars."[15] Elements in the periodic table up to the weight of iron are made in stars. Some stars needed to explode as supernovae in order to provide the temperature and forces necessary to make the rest of the heavier elements required for life.[16]

The coincidences continue. The universe is composed of matter. But this is contradicted by the laws of physics which say that matter and antimatter must exist in equal proportions, canceling themselves out.[17] We should not exist. However, for every one billion anti-protons in the early universe, there were one-billion-and-one protons. The billion pairs annihilated each other to produce radiation, leaving just one proton to build the universe. Why was there more matter than antimatter in this universe? The Kiev experiment being conducted in the United States of America set out to explain this. Researchers suggest that just as there can be imperfect crystals formed during the phase transition between water and ice so, over a long period of time, there can be slight errors in the interaction of matter and antimatter which can result in a slight net gain of matter. The question is, was this discrepancy deliberate? Was this imperfection created on purpose?[18]

Coincidences such as this have even caused Stephen Hawking (the eminent English cosmologist who is ambivalent about faith) to wonder about religious implications. He says, "The whole history of science has been the gradual realization that events do not happen in an arbitrary manner, but that they reflect a certain underlying order, which may or may not be divinely related."[19] For much of his scientific career, Hawking did not discount the possibility of God. He once said, famously, "The odds against a universe like ours emerging out of something like the Big Bang are enormous. I think there are clearly religious implications."[20]

More recently, however, Hawking has shifted his position and suggested that there is now no need to invoke a god to set the universe going. He argues in his book "The Grand Design" that, "Because there is a law such as gravity, the universe can and will create itself from nothing. Spontaneous creation is the reason there is something rather than nothing, why the universe exists, why we exist. It is not necessary to invoke God to light the blue touch paper and set the universe going."[21]

This comment illustrates two things. The first is that people's convictions about science and faith is often a work in progress (as

Darwin's certainly was) and can change with time. Secondly, it illustrates that giants in a particular area of learning are not immune from sloppy thinking when they stray into an academic discipline outside their field of training. Hawking has been rightly castigated for the above comment by many academics including Professor John Lennox, mathematician and Christian apologist at Oxford University, who responded to Hawking's claim, saying:

> Contrary to what Hawking claims, physical laws can never provide a complete explanation of the universe. (Such) laws do not create anything in and of themselves. ... What Hawking appears to have done is to confuse law with agency. His call on us to choose between God and physics is a bit like someone demanding that we choose between aeronautical engineer Sir Frank Whittle and the laws of physics to explain the jet engine.
>
> Hawking's argument appears ... illogical when he says the existence of gravity means the creation of the universe was inevitable. How did gravity exist in the first place? Who put it there? And what was the creative force behind its birth?[22]

The physicist and cosmologist, Paul Davies, who holds to no conventional faith, agrees with the earlier sentiments of Hawking in suggesting that faith in God is scientifically reasonable. He says:

> A careful study suggests that the laws of the universe are remarkably felicitous for the emergence of richness and variety. In the case of living organisms, their existence seems to depend on a number of fortuitous coincidences that some scientists and philosophers have hailed as nothing short of astonishing ... This causal order does not follow from logical necessity; it is a synthetic property of the world, and one for which we can rightly demand some sort of explanation.[23]

Clearly, there are mysteries surrounding the order of the universe that require explanation.

A RELATIONAL UNIVERSE

Further evidence that intelligent life was planned comes from our unexpected ability to do science and understand the universe. Why can we do science at all? Where do we get this marvelous power to understand things? Paul Davies says: "What is remarkable is ... that the human mind has the necessary intellectual equipment for us to 'unlock the secrets of nature.'"[24]

Polkinghorne echoes the same sentiment and marvels that the universe is so astonishingly open to us and rationally transparent to our inquiry. He suggests that the fact that we understand the subatomic world of quantum theory and the cosmic implications of general relativity goes far beyond anything that could conceivably be of relevance to survival fitness.[25] Ours is a universe that is deeply intelligible to us, a universe which allows mathematics to unlock its secrets. This remarkable feature requires an explanation. Theism, Polkinghorne suggests, provides just such an explanation. "If the universe is the creation of a rational God, and we are creatures made in the divine image, then it is entirely logical that there is order in the universe and that it is accessible to our minds."[26]

ORDER IN SURPRISING PLACES

Physicists and mathematicians have not only wondered why equations of the laws of nature must be beautiful but why equations in mathematics can themselves produce unexpected beauty.

Mathematicians occasionally use equations to draw pictures. However, they have been staggered by the fact that equations that they might reasonably expect to draw chaotic pictures or very simplistic pictures can actually produce beautiful, binary symmetrical, organic-looking pictures that have the additional property of being infinitely magnifiable. In other words, these pictures behave as fractals. (A fractal is an entity which is the same regardless of scale, e.g., tree trunks divide like limbs which divide like branches which divide like twigs.) The best known fractal used to find the value of constants to produce such pictures is the Mandelbrot set, named after the person who discovered it.[27] The following pictures illustrate the Mandelbrot set and some of its remarkable properties:

Cosmic Order as Evidence for God 59

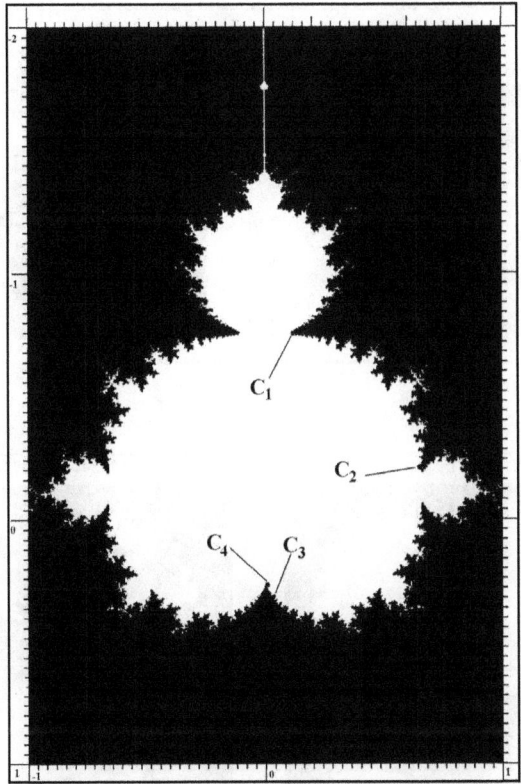

Note the four points C1, C2, C3, and C4. If these values (or any others from the edge of the Mandelbrot pattern) are used as a constant in the Mandelbrot equation, it will result in other patterns being produced.

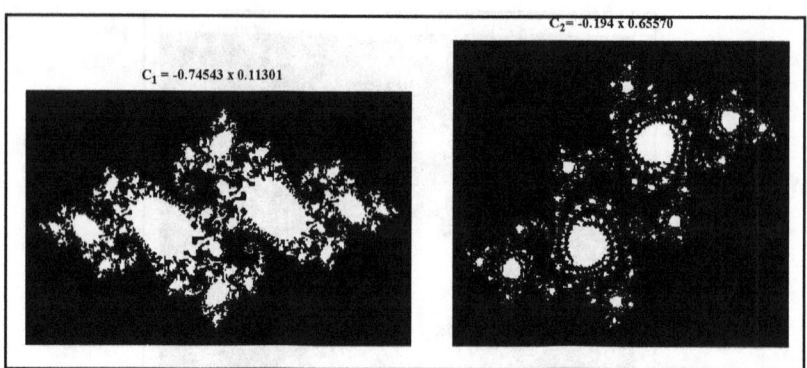

C1 and C2

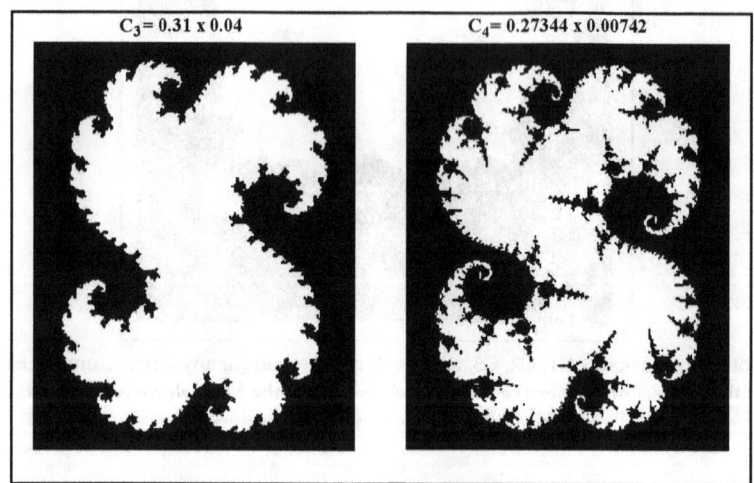

C3 and C4

If the pattern C4 is examined more closely, it will be discovered that the pattern is infinitely magnifiable, being limited only by the power of the computer used to generate the pattern.

Cosmic Order as Evidence for God   61

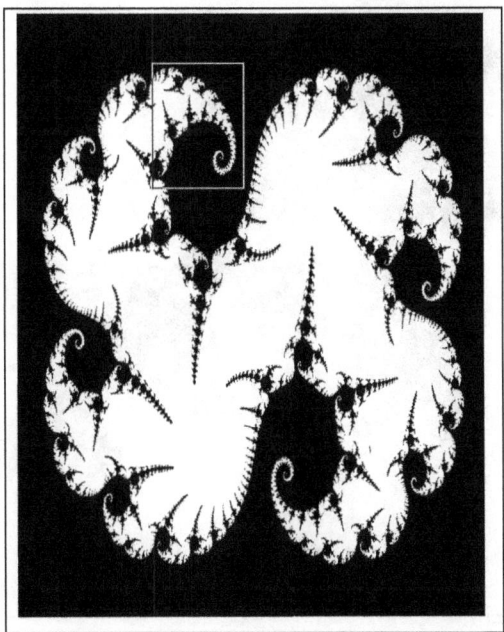

Note the section seen in the box. This (or any other section) can be infinitely enlarged (limited only by the power of the computer) —see next picture:

And if the tiny section indicated by the arrow is enlarged; this is the result.

And if the tiny section
indicated by the arrow is enlarged; this is the result.

Is the fact that we find order in surprising places significant?

From what we observe, the universe appears remarkably ordered, open to rational inquiry and finely tuned to allow for the existence of life forms such as humankind. As Polkinghorne says, its rational beauty and rational transparency, is shot through with signs of mind.[28] The Christian philosopher John Leslie believes that it is just as reasonable to seek an explanation of anthropic coincidences as it would be reasonable to ask why a man who said his fishing apparatus could only accept fish exactly 23.2576 inches long, when casting his rod into the lake, instantly catches a fish of that exact size. This leads Leslie to conclude either that God is real or that there must be a huge number of varied universes, of which a few could be ordered purely by chance.[29] Let us, therefore, look at the alternatives to God being responsible for our ordered universe and examine other possibilities, including the existence of many and varied universes.

CHALLENGES TO THE ANTHROPIC PRINCIPLE

Not everyone finds the order of the universe remarkable or the anthropic principle significant. Mathematician and astronomer Bernard Carr and Cambridge cosmologist Martin Rees have two objections to the anthropic principle. First, they say that the anthropic explanation is unsatisfactory because it is only able to comment on the universe after the event of its creation. It cannot be used to predict any feature of the universe.[30]

Carr and Rees are quite wrong, at least in regards to the use of the weak anthropic principle to predict a scientific outcome. There is one very significant case of it being used to predict an extraordinarily precise scientific feature of the universe. This case concerned the discovery of how carbon could be made inside hot stars and it featured the work of Fred Hoyle.

Immediately after the Big Bang (13.7 billion years ago), 75 percent of the mass of the universe was hydrogen and 25 percent was helium. (A few other elements such as lithium and beryllium were present but only in trace amounts.) A number of scientists, including Fred Hoyle, believed that all the elements of the periodic table[31] were built up from hydrogen and helium. Their theory was that clouds of hydrogen and helium collapsed under their own gravitational force to form stars which became nuclear furnaces that began to fuse hydrogen and helium into the heavier elements. These elements, they believed, were then scattered into space when the stars exploded, so seeding the universe with the atomic components of matter, planets and life itself.

The only problem with the theory was that there was no proof of stars synthesizing new elements from smaller component elements. This changed in 1952 when Paul Willard Merrill identified the spectrum of the element technetium in a "red giant" star called R. Andromedae whilst working at the Mount Wilson Observatory. Technetium has no stable isotopes and so is unknown on earth. Even the most stable isotopes, technetium -97 and -98 have half lives of only a few million years which means that this element has long ago vanished from earth over its five billion year history. The fact that Merrill saw the spectrum of the element technetium in red giant stars could only mean that technetium was being made by nucleosynthesis within the star.

Whilst it was now established that stars could cook up heavier elements, no one understood the chemical process that would allow it. In particular, it was not known how hydrogen and helium could combine to form carbon, the element that is the basis of all known living things. The difficulty was due to the fact that every time helium nuclei fused together to make heavier elements, the resultant elements were invariably unstable and decayed immediately back into smaller particles. An added difficulty was that whilst, in theory, it was possible to make carbon-12 by a simultaneous collision of three helium-4 nuclei, in practice, the event would be too rare to account for the amount of carbon that exists in the universe.

Edwin E. Salpeter (who worked with Hans A. Bethe at Cornell University) suggested that carbon might be made in a two step process. Two helium nuclei could fuse to form beryllium-8, then, in the short time before the beryllium decayed, a third helium nucleus could fuse with it to form carbon. However, beryllium-8 is so unstable that it only lasts 10-17 of a second. Even if a third helium nucleus collided with beryllium in this time, it was more likely to blast the beryllium apart than create a carbon-12 nucleus. The beryllium and helium nuclei could only form carbon if the combined mass-energies of beryllium and helium were almost identical with carbon-12. For this to happen, carbon-12 must have a resonance, i.e., a discrete energy state where reaction rate is substantially amplified by quantum effects (much like how opera singers are reputedly able to shatter a glass if they sing at the right frequency). This energy state would need to exactly match the combined mass-energy of the beryllium and helium particles, plus the kinetic energy of their motion. The difficulty was that no such resonance was known to exist for carbon-12.

Fred Hoyle reasoned that because organic life existed, it must be possible to make carbon, and this would mean that a carbon-12 resonance had to exist. He further calculated that the temperature inside a large star would be about 100 million degrees. Knowing this and knowing the masses of both beryllium-8 and helium-4, he was able to predict that an excited state of resonance should exist within the nucleus of carbon-12 which had an energy of 7.6 million electron volts (MeV). Hoyle managed to persuade a research team at Caltech (California Institute of Technology) led by William Fowler to look for this proposed resonant state in carbon-12, and they found it almost exactly at the temperature Hoyle predicted.3 2 So it was that the mechanism of the formation of carbon, the essential component of all life, was discovered.

What makes this discovery interesting is that Hoyle's prediction was a genuine scientific prediction based on the Anthropic Principle. He had said that since he existed as a life form comprised of carbon molecules, carbon resonance at 7.6 MeV had to exist. This discovery rattled Hoyle's atheistic convictions more than any other event. He wrote:

> From 1953 onward, Willy Fowler and I have always been intrigued by the remarkable relation of the 7.65 MeV energy level in the nucleus of C-12 to the 7.12 MeV level in O-16. If you wanted to produce carbon and oxygen in roughly equal quantities by stellar nucleosynthesis, these are the two levels you would have to fix, and

your fixing would have to be just where these levels are actually found to be. Another put-up job? Following the above argument, I am inclined to think so. A common sense interpretation of the facts suggests that a super-intellect has monkeyed with physics, as well as with chemistry and biology, and that there are no blind forces worth speaking about in nature.[33]

The second objection Carr and Rees have to the anthropic principle is that it assumes that the atoms of our periodic table must exist for life to form, and that this may not be the case. However, whilst it is conceivable that other life forms exist, there is no evidence for it.[34] Something with no evidence should not be allowed to cancel out a theory that makes sense of what is (although it should perhaps indicate that the theory should always be open to revision). Carr and Rees realize this and are gracious enough to say that "the anthropic principle is presently the only candidate and it cannot be denied."[35]

Let us now turn to three particular challenges to the idea that humankind might be "special," each of which would suggest we should not attach much significance to the anthropic principle.

THE CHALLENGE POSED BY THE SIZE OF OUR UNIVERSE

Some are not persuaded that humankind is either purposed or significant given the short time we have existed in the universe and the fact that we inhabit such a minuscule corner of it. The philosopher Roland Puccetti is one who suggests that our existence on Earth must be ridiculously insignificant compared to the size and age of the universe.[36] Stephen Hawking also struggles with the claim of the strong anthropic principle that the universe exists to allow intelligent life to develop. He says that whilst our solar system and galaxy needed to be as it is to allow our existence, "there does not seem to be any need for all those other galaxies."[37]

There are those who disagree. For example, John Polkinghorne says that we need not be upset about our apparent insignificance in a vast universe because scientists now understand that a universe as big and as old as ours would be necessary to allow carbon-based life to evolve on any one planet.[38] The size of the universe is necessary to allow the planets and galaxies to be far enough apart to avoid gravitational force clumping them back together before intelligent life could evolve. Time is necessary to allow the universe to be this size. Martin Rees says, "The size of the universe shouldn't surprise us: its extravagant scale is necessary to allow enough time for life to evolve on even one planet round one star in one galaxy."[39]

We might also respond to Puccetti's assertion theologically by asking why he feels time to be so important? Most Christians who believe that God stands outside time, would contend that time is not restrictive to God.[40] They would also say that far from the size of the universe signaling our insignificance, Psalm 19 suggests that it is quite proper that our heads spin in amazement when considering its grandeur for it is meant to show off God's handiwork:

> The heavens declare the glory of God;
> the skies proclaim the work of his hands.
> Day after day they pour forth speech;
> night after night they display knowledge.
> There is no speech or language
> where their voice is not heard.
> Their voice goes out into all the earth,
> their words to the end of the world.
> (Psalm 19:1–4)

It is not true to say that Christians have an over inflated sense of their significance in the universe. What they do have is an appreciation of God's grace to them within the immensity of the universe. C. S. Lewis makes this point when he says: "If it is maintained that anything so small as the Earth must, in any event, be too unimportant to merit the love of the Creator, we reply that no Christian ever supposed we did merit it."[41]

THE CHALLENGE POSED BY INFINITE WORLDS

The possibility that there are an infinite number of universes allowing an infinite number of intelligent life forms to exist could challenge the significance of humankind's existence in our own universe. The possibility of this being the case received support from the theory of "inflationary universes."[42] The first version of this theory was developed in 1979 by Alexi A. Starobinksy of the Landau Institute of Theoretical Physics in Moscow. However, a different version of the inflationary scenario was published in 1981 by Alan Guth, then at Massachusetts Institute of Technology, who knew nothing of Starobinksy's work.[43] Guth had formulated the inflationary theory in order to overcome difficulties that exist with the big bang model of the origin of the universe.

The current big bang theory maintains that the universe was born about 13.7 billion years ago from a tiny cosmological singularity of near infinite temperature and density in which the current laws of physics did not operate. The laws of physics took hold only after the density of the universe dropped below Planck density (10^{94} grams per cubic centimeter). The fiery ball of the universe exploded from this point of singularity and expanded to produce galaxies and stars. Gradually the universe cooled to its current microwave background radiation temperature of 2.7 Kelvins.

Some of the problems with this big bang theory include the fact that the universe is much flatter than that which the theory of general relativity suggests should be the case. Secondly, at the very high temperatures predicted in the very early universe arising from the big bang theory, the universe should contain many super-heavy particles that have only one magnetic pole.[44] The existence of these "monopoles" should be as abundant as protons and make the mean density of our universe 15 orders of magnitude greater than its present value. Thirdly, the big bang theory has difficulty in explaining why matter is so uniformly spread throughout the universe. Fourthly, if the size of our universe is determined by its initial size (given by Planck length) and density (given by Planck density), the universe should only be big enough to hold up to ten elementary particles rather than the billions that actually exist.[45]

Some of these problems can be resolved with the inflationary universe model. This proposes that the universe expanded for a fleeting instant at its birth at a rate much higher than the big bang theory could account for. This period, called the inflationary epoch, was caused by a phase transition when the strong nuclear force broke away from the weak nuclear and electromagnetic forces it was unified with at higher temperatures. This phase transition,[46] thought to have happened about 10-35 seconds after the creation of the universe, filled the universe with vacuum energy in the form of scalar fields.[47] The potential energy of a scalar field caused an exponential expansion of the universe, increasing its size by a factor of 10^{50} in 10-32 seconds until its energy ran out, whereupon the universe continued to expand according to the process of the standard big bang theory.

Andrei Linde proposes that this inflationary process occurs all the time with one universe seeding another so that the universe is, in fact, a huge growing fractal. It consists of many inflating balls (each of which are sub-universes) that produce new balls, which in turn produce more balls, ad infinitum.[48] An interesting aspect of this is that these different sub-universes could be governed by forces of nature that are different from those of our own sub-universe. As each sub-universe cools down, the fundamental forces of nature distill out. As this cooling is somewhat arbitrary, different sub-universes will be governed by different physics. There may therefore exist a "Grand Unified Theory" of which only a fraction may be realized in any one universe. In our sub-universe, inflation has induced the balance of forces which have allowed humankind to develop. These laws of nature were not established from the start but were produced by physical forces. They were not imposed on the universe but are the products of self-organisation.[49]

If this is the case, then there may exist an important consequence. According to the theoretical physicist Lee Smolin, no meaning can be given to a view of the universe from the point of view of an observer who is outside it or who is not a participant in it.[50] This is because they would belong to a universe characterized by different laws of nature which would define the whole concept of knowing. From this, it follows that it is impossible to believe beyond the point of theoretical probability that other universes do or do not exist. Paradoxically, this does not stop Smolin writing, with apparent certainty, a non sequitur saying, "the old idea of an outside creator and knower has served its purpose and may now be relegated to history."[51]

However, notwithstanding its ability to solve some problems, the inflationary theory does create others and is far from a proven theory.[52] It is hoped that NASA's Microwave Anisotropy Probe (MAP) (a satellite launched on the 30th June, 2001) together with observations from the European Space Agency's Planck Satellite might help find answers to the scientific anomalies that remain.

There is possibility that ideology may have played a part in motivating people to postulate the inflation theory. It is worth noting that the initial impetus for the inflationary theory was born in the Soviet Union where there was some antipathy toward the idea of the big bang theory because it too readily suggested the possibility of a creator who started things off. In saying this, it is important not to deny that scientific difficulties do exist with the big bang theory. However, researchers do need to be honest about their own preconceptions when they investigate them. Andrei Linde admits that his work on inflation was partly motivated by ideological difficulties with questions like "who gave the command" for the universe? and "What arose first: the universe or the laws determining its evolution?"[53] By postulating an infinitely existing and becoming inflationary universe, Linde feels these questions are resolved.

In fact, they are not. Meta-questions still exist. On the first page of his book, *A Brief History of Time*, Stephen Hawking recounts a tale where an eminent scientist is challenged by a lady who says that the scientist is wrong in his understanding of the solar-system. She explains that the world is really a flat plate supported on the back of a large turtle. When the scientist asked what the turtle was standing on, the woman replied that it was standing on another turtle, there were "turtles all the way down."[54] We may smile at this naivety but scientists can fall into the same trap. By putting forward the possibility of multi-universes or sequential universes, little is added other than another layer of turtles. The fundamental questions of why the universe is as it is, why we are in it and why we can comprehend it, remain to be solved. To point to an infinite number of universes is simply to point to an infinite number of turtles. Who began the first universe? And why is it that our particular universe (or sub-universe) is so suited to the development of humankind? The physiologist John Eccles makes the point that, "In terms of Natural Theology, it would appear that, in their efforts to escape from a supernatural creation in the Big Bang by a Transcendent God, they had unwittingly proposed continual creation by an Immanent God!"[55]

Polkinghorne reminds us that just the right quantum fields need to fluctuate in order to produce the first inflation with all the necessary forces of nature that will allow intelligent life, and these basic physical laws still need to take specific forms. This fact, he says, needs a better explanation. He also says that the existence of a Grand Unified Theory, of which only a fraction may be realized in any one universe, does not help explain the special nature of our universe. This is because just the right sort of Grand Unified Theory is needed for our universe to exist. What of its origin?[56] Neither does he feel it is very helpful to postulate that myriads of universes could have developed laws of nature to allow the existence of life forms completely unlike our own, therefore making the existence of our laws of nature unremarkable. Polkinghorne says that other forms of life that are not carbon based may exist (perhaps existing as information-processing plasmas[57]), but this is "drawing large intellectual blank check's on unknown intellectual accounts."[58] Certainly, postulating the existence of an infinite number of unobservable universes to explain the existence of our own remarkable universe seems to be a violation of Ockham's Razor which states that the simplest explanation in any set of natural circumstances is probably the correct one. Polkinghorne continues to maintain that the forces, so necessary for the existence of humankind, are not logically necessary and this needs explanation.[59]

It is not easy keeping abreast of the succession of models put forward for the possible existence of many worlds. In fact, the inflation theory is already being challenged by a new theory called string theory (or superstring theory) which also exists in modified form as M-theory. String theory, developed by Ed Witten of Princeton and Paul Townsend of Cambridge, suggests that the four fundamental forces of nature (gravity, electromagnetism, and strong and weak nuclear forces), together with all matter are simply different manifestations of tiny strands or loops of vibrating strings that exist in multidimensional hyperspace.[60] These strings are thought to be a hundred billion billion times smaller than the nucleus of an atom. It is suggested that the particular vibrations of the strings within this multidimensional hyperspace produce all the matter and energy of the universe, e.g., photons, electrons and quarks, etc.

String theory was able to reconcile the two seemingly incompatible pillars of twentieth century physics, quantum mechanics and Einstein's general theory of relativity. According to string theory, the marriage of the laws of large things (Einstein's general theory of relativity) and small things (quantum mechanics) is not only happy but inevitable. However, a complication came when scientists presented no less than five competing string theories. This embarrassment of riches was overcome by postulating the existence of M-theory,[61] a theory that understood the five competing string theories as different versions of the same thing.[62] 2 M-theory considered that all the matter in the universe consists of combinations of tiny membranes rather than strings, and that these exist within 11 dimensions.[63]

The relevance of the concept of M-theory is that it has made possible the idea[64] that the Big Bang might have been caused by the collision of two parallel universes moving through the eleventh dimension. If true, this would mean that time could be traced back to the point of initial singularity and beyond to another parallel world. Whilst M-theory has made the idea of parallel universes a theoretical possibility, it needs to be said that this is merely the latest in a rapid succession of ideas,[65] none of which satisfactorily explain what ultimately started it all off.

Arguments that seek to neutralize the significance of life by setting it in a larger statistical framework are not logically persuasive. Robert Russell is one who is unimpressed with the "many worlds" arguments and does not see in them any logical argument that would deny that life is the en-fleshing of God's intentions and biological evolution is the ongoing expression of God's purposes.[66] Polkinghorne thinks the same and suggests that theistic belief not only gives a better explanation of our ordered existence but also of our experience of life:

> For the theist, the rational beauty of the physical world is not just a brute fact, but a reflection of the mind of the Creator. Aesthetic experience and ethical intuitions are not just psychological or social constructs but intimations of God's joy in creation and of his just will. Religious experience is not illusory human projection but encounter with divine reality. There is an integrating wholeness in the theistic account which I find intellectually satisfying, even though it must wrestle with the mystery of infinite Being.[67]

Caution needs to be exercised by cosmologists when using the term "infinite" to dilute the significance of the existence of humankind. The word "infinite" is not an infinite mental dumping ground that allows any possibility. It is not a magician's hat from which anything can be produced. The astronomer and writer David Darling warns against this sort of thinking when discussing the mystery of how there was once nothing, and then there was a universe. He says, "And the cosmologists try to bridge the two with a quantum flutter, a tremor of uncertainty that sparks it all off. Then they are away and before you know it, they have pulled a hundred million galaxies out of their quantum hats."[68] There is nothing wrong with the concept and use of the word "infinite" if science leads us carefully down that path with its evidence. However, that is the only valid context in which the concept should be used. It is intellectually dishonest to suggest that there are infinite universes that could allow anything—if this is postulated simply to allow people to say that our own ordered universe has no mystery. The fact is, our universe is ordered. Not only that, we can understand it—and these facts call for a more satisfactory explanation.

Another variation of the infinite universes concept is the idea that our universe has continued to grow, die and grow back into existence—and will continue to do so for infinity. Ernan McMullin is one who believes that the "Big Bang" was preceded by the "Big Squeeze" and that the universe has always been expanding and contracting.[69] He does not agree with the likes of Virginia Trimble who describes each successive universe as being completely new, as he argues that, in reality, each universe is seeded from the previous one.[70] McMullin also points to the likelihood that the total mass of each universe will probably remain constant. He says that if this is true, it would indicate that Trimble is not correct in claiming that "what happened before the Big Bang belongs to the realm of pure speculation rather than of physics,"[71] for the constraining parameters occurring at the Big Bang probably determined the size and nature of the universe. These constraining parameters that existed when time began therefore need explanation. It is evident from the above that the infinite worlds concept has not really solved the riddle of the origin of things. Furthermore, there is little to suggest that such concepts are anything more than pure speculation.

THE CHALLENGE POSED BY SETI (SEARCH FOR EXTRA-TERRESTRIAL INTELLIGENCE)

Having considered the challenge to the significance of the anthropic principle that comes from the possibility of there being an infinite number of worlds, let us turn to the challenge posed by the idea that humankind is not special because the universe is teeming with other forms of sentient life.

Perhaps surprisingly, it should be noted that the Christian church has never been universally hostile to the possibility of intelligent life on other planets. Those who have suggested the church has been uniformly hostile to this idea sometimes cite the fact that the Italian philosopher Giordano Bruno (1548–1600) was burned at the stake by the Roman Catholic Church for believing that life existed elsewhere in the universe.[72] In reality, no one knows what the grounds were for his execution as no records exist of his trial. What we do know is that Bruno, an ex-Dominican monk, was contentious in character and heterodox in belief. He was a devotee of Hermetism, a cult which based its teaching on spurious ancient texts allegedly from Egypt which honored Hermes, the Helenised version of the Egyptian god of learning, Thoth. Hermetism was a blend of neoPlatonism (espousing a celestial hierarchy of gods) and pantheism. It also fostered links with mysticism and magic. Bruno's conviction that life existed on other planets was therefore just one of his unusual beliefs.

Bruno lead a nomadic life around Europe, seeking patronage wherever he could find it by teaching, displaying his technique for developing a prodigious memory and entertaining people with magic. He wrote a number of works, including *On the Infinite Universe and Worlds* (1584) in which he expressed his conviction that there were innumerable suns and planets like our earth which were inhabited by life. This has resulted in him being held up as a champion of science who stood up against the church. In reality, he had a poor understanding of astronomy, and although he held to the Copernican model, he disagreed with Copernicanism on many key points. It is likely that he was executed for his unconventional theology rather than for his conviction that life existed on other planets.[73]

The church has actually been considering the theological implications of life on other planets for a long time.[74] Thomas Aquinas was one who declared that our concept of God must be freed from the confines of earthly thinking and allow that God may well have been incarnate in other worlds.[75] His contemporary, the Franciscan theologian Bonaventure (1221-1274), also believed in the possibility of other worlds. He believed that God could have made a time before our time and that such a time could have had its own world.[76] Others in the church expressed a different point of view. The Lutheran theologian Philip Melanchthon (1497-1560) believed that as Christ had appeared and died only once, there could be no intelligent life in other worlds.[77]

The Catholic theologian, Denis Edwards, is a contemporary writer who examined this issue. He suggested that the existence of intelligent life on other planets may well pose problems for traditional Christian theology and gives three reasons why it is not appropriate to assume that God's saving action through Christ can simply be transferred to extraterrestrial communities. The first is that the biblical writers were concerned only with what they knew. They knew nothing of extraterrestrial life. As such, no doctrinal decision of the past should be asked to solve a question that was not asked at the time. Secondly, Jesus of Nazareth appeared in history as a human within a specifically earthly context. Whilst the cross is central, many theologians see that salvation is more than the cross in that it also includes the words, deeds, life and resurrection of Jesus Christ. How could these be translated to extraterrestrials? Thirdly, there may be more to God than the trinitarian understanding God has chosen to reveal to us and, whilst his treatment of extraterrestrials cannot run counter to God's essential character revealed to us, God's ways of being and dealing with other forms of creation may be beyond our comprehension.[78]

Edwards makes the point that the possibility of extraterrestrials being saved by Christ's death on a cross on planet earth depends on one's theological understanding of salvation. Is the significance of salvation mainly Anselm's concept of satisfaction, or is it the Reformation idea of substitutionary atonement, or is it the Roman Catholic idea of sacrifice? If its significance is simply Karl Rahner's idea of it being a symbol of God's saving love,[79] then it could have universal scope even though it found its explicit expression in the Christ event.[80] Some biblical passages suggest we should be careful not to define the ministry of Christ in an exclusively human centered way.[81] Christ was not just involved with the earth in the act of salvation but with all created things (John 1:3; Colossians 1:16; Hebrews 1:2). Non-human life forms on earth are already in a covenant relationship with God (Genesis 9:8–17) and they too are waiting to be made new as a result of Christ's redeeming work (Romans 8:20–22). If intelligent life exists on other planets they could be doing the same.

What can be seen from this debate is that the question of whether or not intelligent life exists on other worlds is a subject about which the church has never had a unanimous opinion.

An examination of the possible consequences of intelligent life existing on other planets might help us understand whether the church should have a firm opinion on this matter. The first possible consequence might be that life on other planets would signify that Christianity was untrue. Humankind is simply one of a myriad of life forms that exist on planets throughout the universe. No Christ figure has ever come to save other (possibly more advanced) life forms on other planets and so Christianity is false.

The difficulties with this possibility are that, first: no sentient life has been seen on other planets; and second: the Christian faith is based on acts in history and is therefore not simply a philosophic concept that can be discarded. Whatever may or may not be discovered, these acts in history will continue to require explanation.

The second possibility is that sentient life does exist on other planets and God has committed himself to love them all in the same way that a mother can love more than one child. If Christ's act of salvation cannot be directly applied to intelligent life of other worlds, then the possibility of further incarnations in other worlds cannot be ruled out.[82] Thomas Paine, a deist, believed this last option to be absurd because he believed there must be so many other worlds in the universe that God would be worn out rushing between them dying for the benefit of its inhabitants.[83] He, perhaps, has a very limiting view of God. It is a logical possibility that God may have been incarnate to other life forms as the Son of God. If this is so, God would not need millions of saviors for there is no reason why the one Son of God couldn't be incarnate in multiple forms. In heaven, all life forms from all planets would co-exist in a spiritual form, all physical forms having being superseded (1 Corinthians 15:35–44). This would enable all life forms to live together in a relationally rich way with God who purposed them all.

The third possibility is that sentient life exists on other planets but that God has only been incarnate on earth. In this case, other life forms that God wishes to have an eternal loving friendship with, may be treated in the same way as people of distant tribes and nations who have never heard the Christian gospel. Yet, through their pious and moral behavior, they may be saved from their own faith position because of the saving work of Christ Jesus on earth. They are included amongst Karl Rahner's "anonymous Christians."[84] This sort of understanding was first articulated by the Franciscan theologian Guillaume de Vaurouillon (c.1392–1463). He believed that Adam's sin would have no effect on people of other worlds but that, nonetheless, Christ's death (still necessary for their salvation) could be redemptive for them.[85] In contrast to this, Timothy Dwight (1752–1817), President of Yale University, made the point that humanity may be the only group in the universe that fell into sin and requires redemption.[86]

What can be concluded is that if intelligent life is discovered on other planets, then that, in itself, does not present insurmountable difficulties to the Christian faith. Apart from the considerations above, the physicist Paul Davies makes the point that if life existed on other planets, it would indicate that life was not so much due to unlikely chance events so much as to the inherent properties of the laws of nature, i.e., it is determined. He suggests that an ingeniously biofriendly universe makes atheism less compelling because it indicates that the guiding hand of God is working through the laws of nature.[87] The fact remains, however, that there is, as yet, no evidence of such life existing anywhere else in the universe. Whilst suppositions should keep us open to new possibilities, they must not have the power to cancel out the significance of our present experience of reality. The very real possibility of humankind being the most advanced life form in the universe needs to be faced.

Scientists continue to be divided over whether or not intelligent life exists on other planets or moons in the universe. One camp, composed mainly of astronomers and physicists, argues that extraterrestrial life must be abundant, whilst the other camp, composed mainly by life scientists, argues that whilst life may exist on other planets, the odds of there being intelligent extraterrestrial life are small.[88] This difference of opinion is illustrated by the fact that the Harvard physicist Paul Horowitz runs a SETI (search for extraterrestrial intelligence) program but the Harvard biologist Ernst Mayer, says that "SETI is a deplorable waste of taxpayer's money."[89] The American Congress seemed to agree for it quashed NASA's SETI program in 1993. The only remaining American SETI programs are privately funded.[90] However, NASA has begun a "search for extraterrestrial life" (SETL), i.e., a search for extraterrestrial life of any form, particularly microorganisms which we are beginning to learn can exist in the extremes of temperature and radiation that exist so commonly in the universe. This is being conducted from the AMES Research Center at Moffett Field, California. Finding an independent evolutionary origin of living matter would discredit the hypothesis that life is an extremely unlikely and rare cosmic phenomenon. As such, SETL has important theological as well as scientific implications.

It has to be said, however, that as yet there is no firm evidence of life in any form existing on any other planet or moon. We have listened to radio waves from space, notably using the giant Arecibo radio telescope in Puerto Rico and examined our own galaxy for other planetary bodies. Many hundreds have been identified, (either because their gravity has caused the star they are circling to wobble or because they have decreased the luminosity of their star when they circled in front of it). Some of these planets are thought to have conditions like those we have on earth. As yet, however, there is no evidence of any life, however primitive, existing on any planet other than our own.

Having said this, it is quite possible for life on earth to have been seeded by life on Mars for it is not uncommon for debris from a meteorite impact to be splashed onto nearby planets.[91] The NASA biologist Imre Friedmann[92] reported that the Martian meteorite ALH84001 (found in Antarctica in 1984) contained magnetite crystals which were arranged in long chains.[93] These could have been formed by living organisms such as magnetotactic bacteria which are found on earth. Scientists had been alert to the possibility of life on Mars because NASA scientist David McKay had announced the existence of possible micro-fossils in the meteorite ALH84001 in 1996.[94] Later, in 1999, he also claimed to find possible micro-fossils in two Mars meteorites known as Nakhla (which fell in Egypt in 1911, killing a dog!) and Shergotty (which fell in India in 1962).

Many scientists discounted McKay's convictions because the supposed fossils were too small to contain the nucleic material necessary for reproduction, as we know it, to occur.[95] They are only 20–100 nanometers in length. However, Dr. Philippa Uwins of Queensland University has recently discovered tiny organisms as small as 2 nanometers which she has called "nanobes" in rock samples from exploratory petroleum drilling cores taken off the west coast of Australia.[96] It is yet to be determined if these nanobes are living organisms. If it is found that they are, then there is a real possibility that life on earth may have been seeded by Martian nanobes traveling to Earth on meteorites.

Today, however, there is a general consensus that the magnetite crystals associated with carbonate globules in the Martian meteorite ALH84001 are not organically derived but are the product of inorganic activity.

Whether or not primitive life began on Mars and was splashed onto Earth, the fact remains that the only place intelligent life is found in the universe to date is on planet Earth. There are also indications that we will never find other intelligent life elsewhere in the universe. The Italian physicist Enrico Fermi (1901–1954) has suggested that if there were colonizing forms of intelligent life, we should have known about them by now.[97] It has been calculated that it would only take about 10 million years to colonize all suitable stars if an intelligent life-form colonized exponentially. This, of course, assumes that they would want to colonize like a virulent virus or had a time-frame long enough to transverse the immense distances of time in order to do so (our nearest star is 4.3 light years away), or that they wanted to communicate with us. Astronomer Jill Cornell Tarter (founding member of Project Phoenix, the SETI Institute's privately funded targeted search for extraterrestrial intelligence) says that the process of two intelligent cosmic life forms contacting each other would take tens of millions of years even for our nearest 1,000 solar-type stars.[98]

Jill Tarter goes on to say that intelligent life would therefore have to be possessed of a stability that is likely to have never had organized religion or who have outgrown it. This pejorative view of religion as something that threatens the stability of a species is a value judgment that does not come from science. It displays her jaundiced view of religious history and completely discounts the possibility that one religion may be true. She also ignores the fact that the U.S.A., one of the world's most Christian nations, has sent a satellite up in space with maps and messages aimed at communicating with other potential intelligent life forms in our galaxy.

Having said all this, it has to be said that the SETI research has yet to turn up anything conclusive and may never do so.[99]

Whatever is discovered, this much is certain: if Christianity is true it will be tough enough to field any scientific discovery. If Christianity is true it will not be like a sickly child that needs to be tucked into bed and protected from the chilly winds of scientific reality. Christianity must welcome scientific knowledge in all fields, including SETL.

One who expressed this view well was Aubrey Moore, an Anglo-Catholic theologian, who wrote in 1891, saying, "Darwinism appeared, and, under the disguise of a foe, did the work of a friend. It has conferred upon philosophy and religion an inestimable benefit, by showing us that we must choose between two alternatives. Either God is everywhere present in nature, or He is nowhere."[100] As such, whilst the possibility of intelligent life existing on other planets would present some difficulties to conventional Christian theology, it would certainly not prove fatal.

CONCLUSION

It is reasonable to conclude that neither the immense size of the universe, nor theories about the existence of other universes, nor the possible existence of life on other planets, are problems that have delivered the coup de grâce to Christianity. The extent to which the universe seems so finely attuned to allow the existence of intelligent life remains a mystery that is reasonably explained by theistic faith. In saying this, theology is not being offered as a rival to scientific explanation but as an understanding which seeks to put science into a wider context within which it can make better sense.

Eighteenth and nineteenth century thinking saw evidence for God from design fall into the "God of the gaps" trap. However, this salutary lesson does not mean we should lurch to the other extreme and have nothing to say about God as a result of our perceptions of reality. If we look at the universe and fail to wonder at its existence simply because we can philosophize about the universe never truly having had a beginning or end, it would stop us from engaging in sensible debate about why the universe we can actually physically measure, exists. Whilst skepticism in science is healthy and wise, a compulsive hermeneutic of suspicion that ignores reality would stop anyone reaching any conclusions, however tentative, about anything. The fact remains that the universe exists, humankind exists and humankind is able to understand much about the universe. These realities deserve explanation.

Scientists and theologians, agnostics and those with theistic faith are all finally forced to a position of faith. This is familiar territory for the Christian who has long understood that their understanding of the universe is an expression of faith (however reasonable it may also be scientifically). The writer of Hebrews makes this plain, saying, "By faith we understand that the universe was formed at God's command, so what is seen is not made out of what was visible" (Hebrews 11:3). Such a position is scientifically reasonable and is held both by Christian scientists like John Polkinghorne as well as scientists like Paul Davies who, although claiming no conventional faith, say that faith in God is reasonable.

> I belong to the group of scientists who do not subscribe to a conventional religion but nevertheless deny that the universe is a purposeless accident. Through my scientific work I have come to believe more and more strongly that the universe is put together with an ingenuity so astonishing that I cannot accept it merely as a brute fact.[101]

So it is that Davies comes to a position where Christians have already arrived. The astrophysicist Robert Jastrow ends his book *God and the Astronomers* by saying:

At this moment, it seems as though science will never be able to raise the curtain on the mystery of creation. For the scientist who has lived by his faith in the power of reason, the story ends like a bad dream. He has scaled the mountains of ignorance; he is about to conquer the highest peak; as he pulls himself over the final rock, he is greeted by a band of theologians who have been sitting there for centuries.[102]

In conclusion, it can be said that it is scientifically reasonable to look for meaning behind the existence of the universe because of the existence of an apparent principle, the "anthropic principle," which states that our universe is precisely ordered in such a way as to allow the existence of humankind. Three challenges to the anthropic principle have been discussed. These have been:

1. the thought that the universe is too big for humankind to think they are significant within it
2. the thought that there are an infinite number of different universes within which humankind must lose any sense of significance
3. the thought that the likely existence of other intelligent life means that the existence of humankind is not purposed in any way.

In response, we can say that the universe needs to be as big as it is to allow sufficient time for it to be old enough to allow life as we know it to develop on any one planet. We have also established that there is, as yet, no firm evidence of there being an infinite number of other universes or of sentient life existing elsewhere. However, if intelligent life did exist elsewhere, it would not necessarily present insurmountable difficulties to Christian faith.

Nonetheless, these issues raise another objection. Whilst observations of apparent cosmic order persuade some of the reasonableness of faith, others struggle to see God because they see too much evidence of chaos and suffering. How can faith take into account not only the order of the universe but also the apparent disorder, happen-stance and suffering seen in the universe? This will be examined in the next two chapters.

4

Cosmic Disorder as Evidence Against God

*The eternal silence of those
infinite spaces frightens me.*

—Blaise Pascal (1623–1662),
Mathematician and philosopher, in *Pensées*, (1670)

On the morning of September 11th, 2001, nineteen terrorists affiliated with al-Qaeda hijacked four commercial passenger jet airliners and crashed two of them into the twin towers of the World Trade Center in New York, killing 2,206 people. This event was the catalyst that prompted Sam Harris, an American graduate in neuroscience, to write a book, called *The End of Faith*, which was critical of Islam and critical of the role of the Christian right in contemporary America.[1] A few years later, he followed this up with a small book called *Letter to a Christian Nation* in which Harris tackled the problem of evil and expressed the difficulty he had in believing in a good God who allowed disasters like Hurricane Katrina.[2] Both books made the *New York Times* best seller list.

Whilst the extraordinary order of the cosmos points many to the possibility of God, it must also be acknowledged that the existence of suffering and random acts of chaos persuade others that no loving God is in control. According to the South Australian questionnaire, 41 percent of people believe this to be the case.[3] In the scientific world, many physicists have pondered the possibility of God because they observe a universe finely tuned to allow the possibility of life. However, biologists such as Jacques Monod and Richard Dawkins, have remained more resistant to theistic belief. This is probably because biologists see the brutal reality of existence played out on planet earth.[4] Whilst physicists marvel at the order of the universe and the beauty of the laws of nature, biologists see life as a lottery, a cruel competition for existence that is careless of suffering and blind to any plans at all, let alone those of a beneficent God. Charles Darwin expressed this view when he wrote to his Christian friend, the distinguished American botanist Asa Gray on May 22nd, 1860, saying:

> I had no intention to write atheistically. But I own that I cannot see as plainly as others do, and as I should wish to do, evidence of design and beneficence on all sides of us. There seems to me too much misery in the world. I cannot persuade myself that a beneficent and omnipotent God would have designedly created the Ichneumonidae with the express intention of their feeding within the living bodies of Caterpillars, or that a cat should play with mice. Not believing this, I see no necessity in the belief that the eye was expressly designed. On the other hand, I cannot anyhow be contented to view this wonderful universe, and especially the nature of man, and to conclude that everything is the result of brute force. I am inclined to look at everything as resulting from designed laws, with the details, whether good or bad, left to the working out of what we may call chance.[5]

Many biologists, therefore, struggle to believe that God exists, or if he does, believe he exists as an unfeeling, absentee landlord.

CHANCE AND DISORDER

The existence of apparent chance and disorder in the universe cannot be ignored. We see it in the harsh realities surrounding the survival of some individuals and species over others. Chance also appears to have been a major factor in determining the very composition of the earth and its ability to sustain sentient life. Examination of moon rocks has shown that the earth and our moon are composed of a similar volcanic rock type. A theory that currently commands respect is that towards the end of the planet-forming period of our solar system, a massive planetesimal[6] the size of Mars smashed into planet earth. The collision was so great that the iron of the planetesimal pushed through into the center of the earth. In doing so, the collision gave the earth its spin (which was probably not a 24 hour cycle as it now is but a cycle of just a few hours long). Meanwhile, molten debris caused by the collision orbited our planet and coalesced to form the moon. Eventually, the rotation of the earth slowed down as a result of tidal friction and, as it did so, the moon's orbit retreated from the earth. By the time complex organisms began to flourish in the Cambrian era,[7] the earth's rotation had slowed to about 19 hours.[8]

If we also consider the possibility that an asteroidal impact 65 million years ago killed the dominant life form, dinosaurs, allowing our miniature primate ancestors space and time to evolve into human beings, this again makes it difficult to ignore the possibility that chance, rather than design, determined the existence of life on earth.[9] How do scientists respond to the apparent agency of chance?

IS THE BLUEPRINT OF LIFE CONTAINED WITHIN SCIENCE?

The incidence of chance events persuades some that God does not exist and that all the features of the universe can be explained scientifically. Such a position is called evolutionary naturalism. This is a belief that blind chance (perhaps operating during the inflation of the universe) has generated the laws of nature which have determined how the universe will work. These laws of nature then allow chance events to develop the life forms that exist in perfectly understandable scientific ways.

Evolutionary naturalism is not a new idea[10] but it was an idea that gained particular impetus with the discoveries of Charles Darwin. Although evolutionary naturalism has had a significant following amongst scientists (particularly biologists) it must be said that not all scientists without theistic faith are evolutionary naturalists. For example, Ursula Goodenough (Professor of Biology at Washington University) is content to allow mystery rather than science to explain some things.[11] Nonetheless, evolutionary naturalism is popular amongst some scientists who see it making sense of the apparent lack of any plan for the universe.

Slightly softer versions of evolutionary naturalism exist which admit that life is a miraculous event, quite possibly initiated by a deity, but those who hold this view still insist that the blind mechanism of evolution then develops the direction life takes. One who expresses this view is the biochemist Christian De Duve. De Duve allows for the miracle of life but not the miracle of humanity. He believes that a deity may be responsible for the laws of nature that drives the evolution of life but that humankind is not the ultimate achievement of evolution. Humankind is simply a chance phenomenon, a transient evolutionary stage. De Duve would therefore struggle with the Christian idea that the existence of humankind was in any way planned by God. His position is that of the "biological determinist" (someone who believes that the emergence of life is an inevitable consequence of the laws of nature).[12]

There are different forms of biological determinism. "Strong" biological determinism suggests that life is written into the laws of physics, i.e., the laws of atomic physics contain within themselves a blueprint for life. The American chemist, Sidney Fox, has claimed that the laws responsible for the formation of peptide bonds in the production of proteins would automatically cause life to develop in the same way that water inevitably forms ice crystals when the temperature drops.[13]

"Weak" biological determinism is a little more modest. It claims that life emerges with a high degree of predictability as a result of the propensity for matter to self-organise.

De Duve, a proponent of strong biological determinism, points out that the human species has much in common with all life, e.g., in the amino acids comprising its DNA and genetic make-up, which suggests that *Homo sapiens* is "one among millions of terminal twigs on the tree of life."[14] This suggests that life arose naturally by way of processes entirely explainable by the laws of physics and chemistry. He therefore says that the idea that life was launched by a special act of creation has no basis for credibility.[15] De Duve believes that there must be many celestial bodies in our galaxy and universe with a similar history to earth and therefore great numbers of opportunities which allow life must exist.

Life is therefore neither special or unlikely. Even the natural variability of biological populations on our own planet suggest that there are a wide variety of possibilities for life.[16]

De Duve is perhaps being premature in pre-empting the findings of SETL (the search for extraterrestrial life). He is confusing the fruitfulness of evolution in allowing living organisms to evolve with the fruitfulness of the universe in its ability to produce life. Whilst there is evidence of the former, there is, as yet, a singular lack of evidence for the latter.

The physicist Paul Davies does not agree with Christian de Duve's strong determinism and says, "There is absolutely no evidence that the laws of physics we know at present contain life, still less intelligence."[17] Christians would agree. Whilst God may indeed use the mechanisms of the laws of nature to his ends, it is not the laws of nature that are inherently creative so much as the God of the laws of nature. The theologian Thomas Torrance reminds us that there is no intrinsic reason why the universe and its laws of nature should exist at all or be what they actually are, hence "we deceive ourselves if, in our natural science, we think we can establish that the universe could only be what it is."[18]

Davies does not say strong biological determinism is impossible, only that if it proves to be the case, it would require the existence of more than the normal laws of physics. He is skeptical that Darwinian selection could have happened at the molecular level, within the primordial chemical soup from which life developed. Davies points out that organic replicating molecules, like ribonucleic acid (RNA), are extraordinarily complex and are unlikely to have formed by chance. He also says that any molecule formed would be required to have exactly the right likelihood of making imperfect copies of itself. These chemical variants would be necessary to fuel the process of chemical selection by evolution. Too much change would be catastrophic as nothing would last long enough to be selected; too little change and the information would leak away faster than natural selection could develop it. This conundrum is known as "Eigen's error catastrophe."[19]

Davies' believes that life is more than physical matter. He reminds us that it is also about information. In fact, he calls life, "an information processing and propagating system."[20] This view is also shared by the biophysicist Bernt-Olaf Küppers who writes: Life = Matter + Information.[21] The issue for Davies is where the information has come from. He believes that to simply talk about chemistry is to confuse the medium with the message. The laws of physics simply map input states into output states, they cannot add information on the way.

Chemist and theologian Arthur Peacocke points out that, given the right conditions, it is possible for newly developed physiochemical systems to transform into complex, self-copying systems. (This was shown to be the case by two Nobel laureates, Illya Prigogine and Manfred Eigen.) However, he, like Davies, says that this does not mean that the mechanism has been found which explains how life came about. Chemicals that form the basis of life would need to survive and reproduce in very specific ways.[22] Whilst it may be relatively easy to make the amino acids (the building bricks of life), building bricks alone do not make a house. They need to be linked together in a very particular order.[23]

Davies wants to attribute both a measure of luck to the formation of key organic molecules but also to say that their formation was also predisposed by laws of nature (perhaps as yet unknown informational laws). His position is therefore a midpoint between chance and inevitability. The relevance of this is that if life is simply the result of chance, the atheism of the biologists Monod and Gould would be entirely reasonable. However, if life does, at least to some extent, emerge as an automatic and natural part of inherently biofriendly laws of nature, atheism becomes less tenable and something like design becomes more plausible.[24] Certainly, the weak determinism espoused by Davies leaves open the possibility of divine action, not only in designing a universe able to produce life, but in directing the form life takes by contributing information. It is therefore scientifically reasonable to believe that humankind and the universe is contingent (dependent) on God. However, how can such a universe be contingent on the Christian God yet also evidence apparent acts of randomness and cruelty?

A UNIVERSE RELIANT ON GOD, WHICH CAN ALSO CONTAIN SURPRISES

The Christian claim is that the universe exists because of God's will. It does not have to exist because of some inherent property of its own but only exists because of God's action. However, this dependency on God does not mean that the laws of nature cannot generate novelty through chance events.[25] Thomas Torrance says that the universe's reliance on God explains why it exists in an ordered rational form. However, he also suggests that God has not only imbued the universe with order but also processes which generate novelty. This idea has been developed further by a number of scientists who are also theologians, including Barbour, Peacocke, and Polkinghorne, who say that the universe is contingent on God but that God has placed within the universe generators of novelty which produce outcomes that not even God has foreordained. This will be examined further in the next chapter.

Torrance says that because God has imbued the universe with both order and processes which can generate novelty, the universe is both orientated towards God (examined in theology) and orientated away from God featuring independent processes (examined in science).[26] This is a key point, highlighting the fact that science alone can never give the complete picture of why things are as they are. Torrance goes on to claim that modern science's concept of contingent order is a direct product of the Christian understanding of the universe being contingent on God. He suggests that if there was only chaos in the universe, it would not be open to rational knowledge.[27] As such, "science must reckon with the fact that the orderly connections which it seeks to trace within the universe cannot be followed through scientifically to any final end for they break off at the limits imposed by space and time."[28] This means that we can never look to science to provide the ultimate answers.

This conviction does not always sit easily with scientists. For example, Paul Davies seems torn in two directions in suggesting both that science may be a surer path to God than theology (even attributing to science many of the attributes of a deity)[29] yet also saying, "It is still not clear that science could in principle explain everything in the physical universe . . . 'ultimate' questions will always lie beyond the scope of empirical science."[30]

Torrance says that it is now hard for science to avoid grappling with the concept of contingency. He says that, "the relentless pressure of its own inquiries has carried science to the very limits of being where it can no longer avoid the question as to initial conditions or the basic relation between concept and reality."[31]

In making the case for theology, Torrance is not suggesting that theology exists independently of science. Whilst they are two different disciplines, there should be harmony between them. He makes the point that God interacts with humankind within physical reality: "It is in and through the medium of space and time that God acts upon man and makes himself known to him."[32] As such, there should be no disjunction between science and faith. In fact, Christian theology must house those basic principles upon which any scientific cosmology must rest if it is to be true to the actual nature of the universe. He goes on to say that it is a serious fault with much modern theology that it has concentrated on history and cut faith off from its involvement with science.[33]

Whilst Torrance's perspectives on contingency are helpful, he can go too far in his zeal to see God behind all that exists in the universe. He suggests that some details of the physical features of creation may identify characteristics of God. Whilst this is true in a general sense (as suggested by Psalm 19:1-4), Torrance goes much further. He claims that the concept of singularity (the dense tiny particle that exploded into the Big Bang) helps many people today appreciate the biblical teaching about the unique, once-for-all-ness of the incarnation of God as Jesus Christ.[34] In reality, it is doubtful that the concept of singularity has helped anyone at all with a theological understanding of Christ. Most people do not even understand what a singularity is, far less draw from it insights into the nature of God. The universe contains things both wonderful and dreadful. Torrance is therefore on shaky ground when he invites people to look at aspects of creation and use them to draw conclusions about God. What would the existence of suffering and evil in creation say about the character of God? We can, nonetheless, draw broad conclusions about the Creator from the order we see in creation. However, it is perhaps unwise to venture beyond this when postulating details about God based on the physical features we see in creation.

Owen Gingerich (professor of astronomy and the history of science at Harvard University) is persuaded that God's hand can be seen in the design of the parameters within which the universe exists. This does not mean the provision of a rigid blueprint so much as the provision of a framework within which sentient life could emerge. In other words, God may ensure a universe that is inherently fruitful but may not specify the type of fruit that develop. As an example of this, he cites the seemingly finely tuned and unlikely events which have made possible the existence of carbon, the basis for all organic life.

Carbon is the fourth most common element in our galaxy behind hydrogen, helium and oxygen. As has been discussed in chapter three, carbon is able to be made when two helium nuclei fuse together to form beryllium which is then augmented by a helium nucleus to make carbon inside a hot star. This process would not be possible, however, if carbon-12 did not have an excitable energy state (or "resonance") that was exactly the same as that of a beryllium atom and a helium nucleus colliding together in the middle of a star.[35] The remarkable thing is that had the resonance of the carbon atom been four percent lower, there would have been no carbon and we would not exist. However, had the resonance of oxygen been half a percent higher, all of the carbon would have been converted to oxygen.[36] As it was, it was just right and the stage was set to allow life to develop but the final form of that life may have been the subject of chance. Gingerich therefore believes that only a partial blueprint is given within which there is scope for the novel and "accidental" to develop the potential fruitfulness inherent in the universe. God may well have intended sentient life (as evidenced by the existence of carbon) without specifying which possible life forms would actually be realized[37] This view is echoed by Polkinghorne who says that whilst the "fundamental potentiality for anthropic fertility was built into the fabric of the universe from the start; its actual form of realization was explored and brought about by the contingency of evolving history."[38]

What, then, can we conclude? We can say that the universe gives evidence both to support the optimism of physicists toward the possibility of God (because they see order in the cosmos) and also the pessimism of biologists toward the possibility of God (because they see the role of chance and struggle). Both of their insights point to aspects of truth. Polkinghorne says that the laws of nature are so designed that they will lead to the development of self-conscious and God-conscious beings. However, the precise form of these beings was not laid down by divine decrees from all eternity but it results from the operations of chance. Evolution therefore results from the interplay of chance and necessity.[39] Authentic "chance" and "happen-stance" are necessary to allow new developments whilst "natural orderliness" is required to allow these new developments to be integrated into an orderly universe.[40] This means that God is neither a physical interventionist poking an occasional divine finger into the processes of the universe nor an absentee landlord. Instead, because the universe is released to "expand and become," God has not just created but is creating.[41] Polkinghorne agrees with Arthur Peacocke that God is the Great Improviser of unsurpassed ingenuity.[42]

Gingerich points out that there is an awesome consequence to understanding that there is an element of innate freedom in a contingent universe. If we are given some freedom to shape the destiny of human civilization, we may have "the freedom and the power to end it through greed, selfishness, and downright carelessness."[43] The element of freedom God has built into creation therefore brings with it the awesome responsibility of choice.

PROCESS THOUGHT

What sort of metaphysical framework would allow God to direct the universe but still allow novelty and chance? One such framework (of which there are a number of variants[44]), is "process theology."

Process theology is rooted in the work of the English philosopher and mathematician, Alfred North Whitehead (1861–1947) who first published his ideas as a series of lectures in 1929.[45] His concepts seem bizarre and are not easy to understand. In essence, Whitehead believes that reality is something that is changing, active and becoming. It is in process. He also believes that reality is made up of "actual entities" or "occasions of experience." Controversially, he believes that molecules and living organisms are all actual entities able to feel or experience. Even atoms are actual entities and are responsive, to a limited degree, at the quantum level.[46] Whitehead suggests that the most basic transaction between actual entities are non-sensory perceptions called "prehensions" or the "feeling of feeling." Entities receive prehensions from preceding entities and so are in relationship with them.

Whitehead suggests that at every new moment, each of us is a new human experience born out of the collective momentary events of self-determination that have occurred in response to preceding entities and the environment. However, we are not simply slaves to the past. We have a degree of freedom that allows us to be creative and add to the sum of influences from the past. In this way, we create something new which, in turn, goes on to inform the future. God ensures the orderly continuation of this process and offers at each step divine options (called "initial aims") which, if followed, would lead to the ultimate fulfillment of each entity. These options are presented by God who lures, leads and urges with love (but who never coerces) creation to a better place.[47] Evil and suffering come about as a result of not following God's directing.

If Whitehead is right and God is seeking to lure events towards a certain outcome, what mechanism does God act on to bring about his purposes? Logic would dictate that God does not simply act through people. To believe this would mean that God was inactive for most of the history of the universe. The universe is believed to be 13.7 billion years old and the earth only about 4.5 billion years old. Whilst life appeared on earth quite quickly (the oldest fossil life forms of algal microfossils and stromatolites[48] are 3.5 billion years old) today's *Homo sapiens* are

94 EVIDENCE OF GOD

very much late comers who, it is believed, made their appearance only 100,000 years ago.[49]

What, then, is the causal joint that God acts on to bring about his purpose in all of the universe if he does not just act on human beings? Is it a divine "top down" imposed action, e.g., the just right provision of information, or is it a "bottom up" agency that sees God acting through the world of quantum uncertainty?[50]

Polkinghorne says that those who have proposed that God might work through the agency of quantum uncertainty do not make it clear how these small changes work out in the macro world.[51] He suggests that a possible arena for God's action might be located in the world of chaos theory. Chaos theory teaches that everything in the universe is interconnected. This means that the slightest change in the initial condition of a system can result in a completely different and unpredictable consequence. This phenomenon came to the attention of Edward Lorenz, a meteorologist at MIT who was studying weather patterns. In 1961, he typed in the weather parameters based on 12 equations (that expressed relationships between factors such as temperature, pressure and wind speed) to replay a former weather sequence he was modeling However, the computer did not duplicate this weather sequence as before. In fact, an entirely new sequence was produced. The reason for this was the tiny detail of the computer calculating the sequence using numbers with three decimal places rather than the six decimal places originally used.

This immense sensitivity to initial conditions has given rise to what is known as the "butterfly effect," a name which came about as a result of the proposition that a butterfly stirring its wings over Hong Kong could initiate a chain of events that could affect the course of a tornado in Texas.[52] However, "chaos theory"[53] is really a misnomer because mathematics has discovered that some outcomes occur more often than others in chaotic systems. These favored outcomes have been dubbed "strange attractors." Polkinghorne puts forward the idea that "strange attractors" might be the sites God acts on to bring about his desired outcome.[54] This, says Polkinghorne, would allow both genuine novelty and unpredictable changes, yet also load the odds in favor of particular new developments.

How valid is Polkinghorne's idea? Theologically, most Christians would want to say that God is a God of more than chaos theory. God, almost by definition, must be able to act at every level of creation. There is nothing outside of God's lordship. Sub-atomic particles through to human beings are subject to God, otherwise God is not truly God at all. To look for a single causal joint that God acts on in creation may therefore be unwise. Further, to look for physical causal joints will be futile if the causal joint is not physical but spiritual.

Whilst we should not give up searching for causal joints on which God may act we must (if we are to avoid the trap of lazily ascribing to God those things we do not understand) be mindful that God is likely to be acting at all physical levels, and, quite possibly, at a spiritual level we have yet to understand. The risk one takes by viewing God only through a scientific lens is that God will be reduced to being little more than the intelligence behind the laws of physics. For example, the author and scientific historian Steven Dick is one who wants to consider God as being a "natural" God, the intelligence behind the laws of physics, rather than a "supernatural" Christian God who is also beyond physics.[55]

It is evident that although process theology is a bold attempt to make sense of both the order and disorder we see in the universe, it has very real shortcomings. One of the features of process theology is its claim that even though there is one aspect of God that is perfect and never changes, there is another aspect of God that does change, and that is God's experience. Creativity enriches all life, including the Divine Life itself. In this way, God is dependent on, and changes with, the temporal process. God and creation cannot be divorced, as Whitehead explains:

"It is as true to say that God transcends the World, as that the World transcends God. It is as true to say that God creates the World, as that the World creates God."[56] Process theologians therefore believe that God is "becoming" as God journeys with humanity through evolutionary history. God is described as being dipolar, both constrained by time and the creative surprises of history and beyond time so that he knows its ultimate outcomes. God is therefore both temporal (deeply engaged with historical process) and atemporal.[57]

A difficulty with understanding that God is "becoming" as God journeys with humanity through evolutionary history is that God is dependent on humanity in order to become. This would mean that God's creation of humankind was not a free act, for God needs us in order to fully be who he is. Some process theologians such as the Quaker, Grace Jantzen,[58] even suggest the analogy that the relation of God to creation is the same as that of human beings to their bodies. One requires the other. However, such an understanding would violate the Christian understanding that God's creation of the universe was not a necessary act but a chosen free act of grace. God is not constituted by us or dependent on us for identity or nourishment in any way.

Ian Barbour is a panentheist who believes that God penetrates the whole universe in all created matter—but is more than the universe. Barbour is also a noted exponent of process thought. Whilst he does not think Whitehead's process theology allows for the radical diversity needed to fuel the genuine novelty we see in evolutionary history,[59] Barbour nonetheless adopts process thinking and suggests that God's action in the universe is one of luring creation in a certain direction.[60] He speaks of a God of persuasion, rather than compulsion, who "influences the world without determining it."[61] Barbour is honest enough to point out an obvious difficulty with this understanding which is that it calls into question "the traditional expectation of an absolute victory over evil."[62] Process thinking calls into question God's omnipotence, and must therefore allow that humankind is vulnerable to an uncertain future. This is very different from the Christian conviction that God will have the final word.

Scientist and theologian Arthur Peacocke is also a panentheist. He too speaks of God presiding over the universe's "propensity for increased complexity"[63] directing it towards certain outcomes. A difficulty with this, though, is that there is no evidence that the place God is directing us to is in any way better or more godly than the place we have come from. We might be forgiven for thinking that if God is directing events, God seems to have directed a lot of evil. Whilst some might protest and say that the loving altruistic behavior of some humans is evidence enough of a divine direction, the social biologist Edward O. Wilson would argue that this is not necessarily the case. He believes that altruistic behavior can be explained by Darwinian selection in that such acts enhance the survival of close relatives with similar genes, e.g., in an ant colony. Selective pressures would encourage such self-sacrifice. As such, he, like Dawkins, believes that all human behavior can be explained by evolution.[64]

John Polkinghorne is one who disagrees with Barbour's panentheistic form of process thinking. Polkinghorne sees no evidence of divine control over the huge and variable dynamics of the physical world.[65] He also says that process thinking "gives an inadequate account of divine action, which seems to be restricted to the role of a powerless pleading from the margins of occurrence."[66] Polkinghorne suggests that in reacting against a God seen as a dominating Cosmic Tyrant, process theologians appear to have settled for a "Marginal Persuader."[67] Polkinghorne's other difficulty with process thinking is that the process of cosmic and biological evolution is not even (as might be expected if God was continually involved) but goes forward in jerks.[68] This objection is perhaps less convincing as there is no reason why God could not be a God of jerky advances every bit as much as smooth ones.

Despite Polkinghorne's rejection of process thinking, he does seem to flirt with concepts not unlike it. He suggests that God may "not yet know the unformed future. History unrolls, rather than just existing. We make the future; it is not up there waiting for us to arrive."[69] This, of course, is consistent with his understanding of contingence. However, he goes further. He believes that there is room for our action in the world as well as God's action and that the way we act is through prayer. When we pray, "we offer our room to manoeuvre to be taken by God and used by him in the most effective way in relation to his room for manoeuvre."[70] This suggests that each human being has a quota of "prayer power" which, if enough is added to God's power, might determine a cosmic outcome. Again, this would seem to suggest that God is not omnipotent and that the future is as equally uncertain as the process thinkers would have us believe.

Process theology and similar forms of thinking therefore have their shortcomings. Perhaps a better understanding of reality can be obtained if we allow a greater input from orthodox theology. If this is done, God is released to be more than a "marginal persuader" in the universe.

THE NEED FOR INPUT FROM CONVENTIONAL THEOLOGY

If Christianity is right, trying to apprehend the truth about God through science alone must appear foolish if God has chosen to be known primarily through his self-revelation as the Trinity. It is important to remember that this self-revelation is not an unearthed philosophy but is based on acts in history that have been reflected on theologically. As such, Christians cannot easily be asked to give it up in favor of a speculative philosophy based on science. To do so would be asking them to turn their backs on knowledge. Having science dialogue with theology does not mean that theology gets thrown out of the window. If orthodox theology is discarded, it will not just be bad for theology, it will be bad for truth. The challenge for us is therefore to allow the two disciplines to enrich each other and constrain each other, helping each other to remain honest to their own disciplines. Only when each discipline opens itself up to be informed by the other will we have true consonance.

At the moment, there seems to be little consonance between process thinking and the more conventional Christian theology of the German theologian Karl Barth. Barth begins his magisterial work *Church Dogmatics* with a discussion of the Trinity. He does this because Barth's metaphysical framework is uncompromisingly based on the trinitarian nature of God, i.e., that the one God exists in community within himself of Father, Son, and Holy Spirit. Barth's central tenet is that God "reveals Himself through Himself."[71] Revelation of God is not found in nature or in human self-consciousness or any other subjective human experience but in Jesus of Nazareth. Barth goes on to make it very clear that God's creation, redemption and self-revelation are free acts. Unlike that suggested by process theology, God does not become more or less God by creating and does not need us or creation in order to be fully God. "God is free to reveal Himself or not to reveal Himself. God's self-unveiling remains the act of sovereign divine freedom."[72]

What is science to make of this claim that God's chosen self revelation as Trinity is foundational to any right understanding of reality? If true, scientists would be foolish to design a metaphysical framework which does not take this into account. Equally, theology would be foolish not to allow its discipline to be enriched by science. Polkinghorne says that theology needs to "avail itself of their answers in the conduct of its own inquiry, thereby setting them within the most profound context available. Theology's regal status lies in its commitment to seek the deepest possible level of understanding."[73] Theology is therefore not simply looking at the physical world for hints of God's existence but is looking to God's existence as "an aid for understanding why things have developed in the physical world in the manner that they have."[74]

Christianity therefore appreciates that science helps us understand the role of chance in allowing the fruitful exploration of potentials in the universe, and that the cost of this is death, impermanence and suffering. Christianity also appreciates, however, that scientific explanations are too harsh and sterile to make sense of the whole experience of existence, for it points only to cause and effect rather than purpose and meaning.

In conclusion, it can be said that Christianity has to take seriously both the evidence for order and the evidence for chaos and suffering in the universe. Evidence suggests that it is reasonable to hold to a position of "weak determinism." Weak determinism leaves open the possibility of a universe that is contingent on God but which must also generate novelty and experimentation in order to fuel its development. Whilst this experimentation results in a fruitful universe, it comes at a fearful cost, the cost of competition, waste and suffering. Attempts to insist that God is still actively involved in times of suffering by proposing the science based philosophy of process thought are not persuasive. We need more help from conventional theology if more convincing answers are to be found to the question of why God created a world in which so much evil, chaos and suffering exist.

The nature of this help is the subject of our next chapter.

5

Theology Completes Science

> Upon this gifted age, in its dark hour,
> Falls from the sky, a meteoric shower
> Of facts—they lie unquestioned, uncombined.
> Wisdom enough to leech us of our ill
> Is daily spun; but there exists no loom
> To weave it into fabric.
>
> —Edna St. Vincent Millay 1892–1950,
> from the poem "Upon This Age"

THEOLOGY IS NOT ONLY compatible with science but also completes the picture of God that science can begin to paint. It is important to complete the picture, for if our concept of God was informed only by science, it would describe a God who was distant, careless of suffering and careless about which species would ultimately win the race to become self-conscious, worshiping beings. The vastness of the universe and humankind's recent existence relative to the age of the universe would seem to suggest that God has not particularly planned for the existence of humankind. Science would suggest that we are merely a chance phenomenon, one of an infinite number of possible outcomes that will blossom for a brief while in history. Science alone might prompt us to believe that God was only present to start things off and thereafter, sat on his hands wondering what his universe would produce. And if this is the case, how could God be committed to love something so unforeseen as humankind? Is Christianity wrong?

John Polkinghorne is strident in his insistence that God is not just a necessary being to "start things off," something he has future reproved

Theology Completes Science   101

Stephen Hawking for suggesting. Hawking had written, "So long as the universe had a beginning, we could suppose it had a creator. But if the universe is completely self-contained, having no boundary or edge, it would have neither beginning nor end; it would simply be. What place, then, for a creator?"[2] Polkinghorne insists that God is not just required to create and begin things but that God is also necessary to sustain the universe. As such, every moment is a moment of creation. The question is, what is it that God wants to sustain? Does God know? Does God care? Does God have a specific objective in mind and, if so, is humankind part of that objective? How "in charge" can God be if God is present only to "sustain" a giant game of chance?

The cosmologist and author Timothy Ferris is one who does not believe that humankind was pre-planned by God. He speaks of "cosmic evolution" and observes that this evolution seems to be genuinely creative in that its products cannot be predicted.[3]

Ferris needs to exercise care when using the term "evolution." Cosmic evolution cannot work in the same way that biological evolution is said to be responsible for increased biological complexity. Biological evolution is driven by the natural selection of traits that best help an organism to thrive. However, in the vastness of the universe, there seems no obvious mechanism to fuel evolution and allow for the selection of modes of planetary existence. The fact that Ferris uses the term "evolution" highlights the struggle scientists have when viewing the order of the cosmos without understanding the source of the mechanism that drives it. If cosmic evolution is found to exist, it will obviously not be fueled by genetic mutations which are selected for in biological organisms. We would therefore need to discover a completely new mechanism of evolution that would work at a cosmic level. Rather intriguingly, if this were to happen, we might also need to allow that this mechanism could operate alongside the Darwinian evolutionary model in living organisms.

Because Ferris believes that the outcomes of "cosmic evolution" cannot be predicted, he struggles to believe God is directing any scenario. He observes the key role chance seems to play in mutations and natural selection (as well as its possible role in determining inflationary universes) and asks what role there can be for an omniscient creator?[4] However, in saying this, Ferris may be guilty of confusing the mechanism with the cause. One might ask what it is that drives the mechanisms of chance that result in sentient life? He seems to acknowledge this himself, for he also says: "Yet there is something enthralling about the undeniable consideration that the universe is not . . . shambling down the entropic slag heap. (Evolution) evidently runs on random chance, yet we can never be certain that what appears to be chance is chance."[5]

Ferris prefers to believe that God wanted nature to produce surprises, phenomena that he could not have foreseen, and suggests that the agency of God's creativity (which so spectacularly reverses the dreary slide of entropy) is "life."[6] In saying this, Ferris may again be confusing ultimate causes. It is not that life is creative but that life is an expression of God's creativity. Ferris also needs to remember that there was considerable creativity in the cosmos which existed well before organic life came about. To point to life as the agency of creativity is therefore inadequate.

In the light of Ferris' understanding, it is not surprising that he concludes that God would betray no trace of his presence in a creative universe, since to do so would rob the creative forces of their independence. He therefore claims that God's language is silence.[7]

Can God's relationship with us only be one of silence? Obviously, the Christian would not agree for when Christology is taken into account it is discovered that God has been far from silent but has spoken to us most significantly through his Son (Hebrews 1:2). When God's revelation in Christ is factored in, it must have a significant effect on how we understand life's great conundrums, particularly why suffering and death exist alongside order and precision in the universe.

Death is seen by scientists as an essential tool, a mechanism which allows the universe to develop increasingly adapted life forms. Arthur Peacocke says that new things can only emerge in a finite universe if old patterns dissolve to make room for them. There is therefore a structural logic about living organisms dying.[8] Death is essential if a species is to be able to adapt to environmental changes and evolve. As such, scientists do not see death as a consequence of sin (Romans 6:23) but as a necessary phenomenon which allows a species to develop. Peacocke says we therefore appear to be "rising beasts rather than fallen angels."[9]

However, it may not be necessary to set the scientific view of death against the theological understanding of death being a consequence of sin. It is quite possible for death to allow the growing complexity of life but for this mechanism to be regretted as something imperfect, a consequence of sin. As we live within the universe, we can only see the fruitful necessity of death because we cannot conceive of another system that would allow the development of a species. This of course does not mean that a better system does not exist within the mind of God.

It is, perhaps, curious that people complain about death given that death is so necessary. Why is this? We complain, because there is a deep intuition of hope within the human spirit which revolts against the nihilistic idea that death has the last word and that there is no meaning to our lives beyond it.[10] We complain about it because we are relational beings rather than throwaway temporary "things." Something in us stubbornly reacts against the idea that we are a transient biological life form, "a poor player that struts and frets his hour upon the stage and then is heard no more."[11] Is this merely a reflection of our neurosis and inability to accept our mortality or does our reaction against such an idea point to a greater meaning?

Although science can point to design and order in the universe and conclude that there is evidence of the possibility of "greater meaning," it cannot prove that such meaning exists. Science can only see reality from "below," from the perspective of those within the reality of physical life. As such, it is difficult for science to give any sense of transcendent worth or meaning. It can only give us the chilly physical certainty of our own mortality and finitude. Where, then, does our sense of worth and meaning come from?

WHEN IT COMES TO MEANING, COSMOLOGY IS INCOMPLETE WITHOUT CHRISTOLOGY

If worth and meaning can only be generated from "below," there are really only two alternatives to explain it. The first is to believe that humankind has engaged in self-delusion and that any sense of transcendent worth is merely a self-made placebo developed to cope with the pain of mortality. The other alternative is that God comes from "above," and places within each of us a conviction of worth that witnesses to the existence of divine purpose. This understanding believes that our sense of worth is not simply a product of evolution designed to encourage us to thrive and reproduce, but reflects a bestowed value given by the only one who can guarantee true worth—God. If this claim is right, then it will mean that the science of cosmology can only be of limited use in helping us understand our meaning. It will mean that science is incomplete without Christology (the study of Christ), for science was never meant to be all that we know.

The claim I make is that the Christianity is able to give us a deeper appreciation of the significance of cosmology. Science can only factor in empirical data whereas Christianity is also able to factor in God's revealed plan for humankind. Christianity gives the phenomenon of the anthropic principle a metaphysical explanation. Whilst it is important not to fall again into the trap of "God of the gaps," it can be said that, without God, many of the "big questions" remain a profound mystery. For example: "Why is a child of a particular hominid species on a small planet orbiting a star thirty thousand light years from the center of a routine galaxy capable of discovering the secrets of the universe?"[12] This was something Albert Einstein marveled at, saying, "the eternal (and incomprehensible) mystery of the world is its comprehensibility."[13] Theism makes sense of these questions.

When it comes to understanding our worth and meaning, the only guarantee we have of these things is that God revealed himself to us and came to us as Christ Jesus. This event meant that humankind was more than a brief meaningless point along an evolutionary conveyor belt, as Darwin had feared.[14]

Theologians have not always been good at voicing these perspectives outside their own discipline. Science/theology workshops generally feature a lot of science but rarely discuss Christology and its implications for our understanding of meaning. John Polkinghorne is one who believes that in its eagerness to integrate contemporary science, modern theology too often subordinates all things theological to the scientific.[15] In these days, scientists are beginning to come to theologians for help in understanding the ultimate questions their disciplines are leading them to. To have them being met by theologians who are so unsure of the Christian claims that they can add nothing helpful to science is tragic.

Having discussed death and its challenge to our sense of significance and faith, let us turn to the challenge to faith posed by suffering.

SUFFERING

The world and the universe sometimes seems meaningless and cruel. The fact that the universe is destined to end (probably in low level radiation) makes the scenario of its existence appear pointless.[16] The specter of suffering seems to confirm the idea that no loving God is in control.

Charles Darwin was one whose experience of suffering caused him to baulk at the idea of the existence of a beneficent God. As we have already discussed, he could not reconcile his observations of suffering with the existence of the Christian God of love. If science is to make sense of this, it needs more help from theology.

Suffering occurs for many reasons but it essentially comes from two sources. It comes as a result of moral evil and it comes from the inherent dangers present in our physical world. The suffering that comes about as a result of moral evil is perhaps easier to understand. Christians believe that the world has been corrupted by our sin (Genesis 3:9–19; Galatians 6:7–8), our lack of wisdom i.e., our bad choices (Galatians 6:7), and Satan (Luke 13:16). The reason why God allows suffering that is the result of moral evil is because true love allows people the freedom to choose their actions and their loyalties. Freedom therefore has its risks. God gives us freedom to make our own choices, and risks that we will make bad choices and suffer the consequences of them. In other words, whilst the will of God is perfect, the way of humankind is not.

However, the suffering caused by the inherent dangers of living in a physical world are less easy to understand. It is a fact that some children die of cancer. It is a fact that a submarine earthquake in the Indian Ocean killed 229,866 people on the 26th December, 2004. It is a fact that fifteen thousand people were killed in Lisbon during an earthquake on All Saints Day (November 1st) in 1755.[17] Many were killed in churches when they collapsed upon them. Could not God have organized it so these things did not happen?

WHAT SCIENTISTS (WHO ARE ALSO THEOLOGIANS) ARE SAYING ABOUT SUFFERING

Peacocke, Barbour, and Polkinghorne all speak of the necessity of the universe being able to generate authentic novelty to allow the inherent fruitfulness of the universe to be explored. Peacocke stresses the essential role of chance in the exploration and expression of the universe's potentialities. He says that God creates through the whole process of law and chance, not just by intervening during gaps in the process.[18] Peacocke suggests God is immanent within the epic of evolution but works within naturalistic powers. God works by "top down" direction in that God determines the parameters that have resulted in life. However, says Peacocke, the cost of such evolutionary complexity is pain and suffering, for an evolutionary world must involve both predation and death. This cost of suffering is therefore something which we and God must bear.[19]

Ian Barbour has, as we have said, largely adopted the thinking of process theology and suggests that the universe is incomplete and is still coming into being.[20] God is not responsible for suffering but is limited by the fact that he is committed to communality. This means that he will seek to persuade, rather than coerce, existence along certain pathways. When the world fails to go down those pathways, God shares in the resultant suffering with us. Barbour goes on to say that the emergence of higher levels of consciousness will inevitably result in a greater capacity for suffering. However, this is not a bad thing for suffering contributes to moral growth (Romans 5:3).[21] Courage would be impossible without danger and temptation. Free choice for good would be meaningless without the option of evil.[22] In suggesting this, Barbour does not, perhaps, adequately address gratuitous evil which appears so unnecessary, even Satanic.

John Polkinghorne seeks a middle way between classical theology and process theology. He seeks to steer between the idea of a God who has love without power, i.e., is an impotent spectator, and God who has power without love, i.e., is a cosmic tyrant. Polkinghorne suggests that God interacts with creation but chooses not to overrule its divinely granted freedom to be itself. This continuous interaction means that God is continuously creating, possibly by inserting pure information to the causal nexus of creation which may be found amidst the murky uncertainties of the quantum world.[23] Polkinghorne says that God is a rational God and that created order is a package deal where its existence and creativity require change and risk. For example, mutations can occur quite spontaneously in the reproductive cells of animals which may be lethal to them or, alternatively, make them better adapted to their environment. He says, "Exactly the same biochemical processes that enable cells to mutate, making evolution possible, are those that enable cells to become cancerous and generate tumors You cannot have one without the other."[24]

> We are part of a physical universe with all its creativity and danger. God is neither following a rigid blueprint nor abandoning existence to look after itself. Rather, the universe has been encoded by God to make itself and evolve self-conscious worshiping beings. Physical suffering and evolutionary blind alleys are the necessary cost of this fruitful complexity.[25]

These scientists all suggest that although God has a definite endpoint in mind, i.e., the creation of self-conscious worshiping beings, the day to day process of God achieving that end is not predictable and may even be unknown to God. We have discussed Process Theology that sought to give this sort of understanding a metaphysical framework. However, this understanding has significant shortcomings. Is there, then, another theological understanding that might take better account of the biblical witness yet also allow for the fact God may not know the future in day to day detail?

SUFFERING AND THE OPEN VIEW OF GOD

Recently, a new proposal for understanding the nature of God has been advanced. It is variously known as the "open view of God," "free will theism," or "open theism." This understanding has not been prompted by science but has come about as a result of theological reflection on issues of freewill, suffering and the role of intercessory prayer. Its interest for us lies in the fact that open theists advance the idea that God may not foresee the future in all its detail. This view, arrived at through theological reflection, is in accordance with that arrived at by some scientists who, through their scientific observations, also conclude that God does not know the future. As such, open theism deserves investigation.

Open theism, popularized by Clark H. Pinnock, John Sanders, and Greg Boyd,[26] proposes that God has chosen to limit his power so that he is able to engage in a reciprocal way with people on a day to day level. God has not locked everything into place by a foreordained plan. He has chosen to share with humankind the task of crafting the events of each day, for God has placed himself in a position where he can be persuaded to, or dissuaded from, a course of action through prayer. God therefore invites us to participate with him in bringing the future into being. This means that whilst God has firmly and unequivocally set in place eventual end-points and goals which must happen, God may not know the details of the future on a day to day basis.

God, therefore, did not foresee the terrorist attack on the World Trade Center on the 11th of September, 2001 and is therefore not culpable for allowing it. The attack was simply the terrifying price of the refusal of humankind to live cooperatively in a bilateral relationship with God. Even though God knows the infinite varieties of the future and also knows past human behavior so that he can well predict the odds of a future event, God still did not know for sure what these terrorists would do. Our relationship with God is an open one, dependent on what we do and what God does in response to what we do.

Open theists stress that God's inability to know the future in detail is a freely chosen, partial, temporal condition. As such, it does not threaten God's omnipotence because God, in his omnipotence, can sometimes choose not to know. As Boyd says, "The future is settled to whatever extent the sovereign Creator decides to settle it."[27] Not everything God wants can be thwarted by human freedom. For instance, they argue that the fact of Christ's coming again is not dependent on us although we can both hasten or delay Christ's return by our actions (2 Peter 3:9,12).

Although open theism has areas of similarity with process theology (in that both allow that the future is not foreknown or foreordained by God in all its detail), Pinnock is keen to distance himself from it. Unlike process theology, he insists that open theism has a biblical basis. He also insists that although God can be and is affected by creatures, as is the case in process theology, unlike process theology, God does not change in his own essential being but only changes in the way he feels and acts in response to our input.[28]

Open theists challenge the concept that God is impassible (incapable of suffering) and omniscient (knows all things) by appealing to biblical witness.[29] However, the difficulty with biblical witness is that it is both supportive of the classical view of God's foreknowledge (1 Samuel 15:29; Malachi 3:6; James 1:17) as well as God's flexibility toward future actions (Genesis 18:23–32; Exodus 32:14; 1 Kings 2:1–4).

How persuasive, then, is the argument that God can choose not to know the future? Is this ability a property of God? If it is, could God also employ it at a cosmic level and also choose not to know the future except for those things God chooses will happen. This would certainly help explain the apparent existence of the role of chance in developing authentic novelty in a potentially fruitful universe. Timothy Ferris could therefore be quite right in suggesting that things happen at a cosmic and biological level that even God cannot predict.

We need to be careful that we do not press open theism for too much when considering its possible application to things cosmological. Its relevance is entirely restricted to helping us to establish whether or not God cannot know the future. It is not possible to go further than this. This is because open theism makes it clear that God's motive for not knowing some of the details of the future is love of humankind. God, in his love, invites humankind to work with him in fashioning the future. Obviously, the same sort of relational motive for not knowing the future details of the universe before life came into being, would not exist. This is because the inanimate elements of the universe are incapable, as far as we know, of a mutual, loving relationship with God.[30]

Proposing the idea that God can choose to be less than himself (in choosing not to be omnipotent because he chooses not to know the future) presents a logical difficulty. Can God choose to be less than he is? Can God choose not to know aspects of the future? Would this ability mean God is particularly omnipotent or would it mean that God is less than omnipotent? In terms of logic, the problem is this: can A be non A?

Whilst suggesting that God is non A (not omnipotent regarding time), open theists do not want to deny that God is also A (omnipotent). Open theists are saying that God is omnipotent but chooses to express it by limiting himself in his ability to see all the future in detail so that he is able to craft the future in partnership with humankind. Certainly, the idea that God is not omnipotent regarding time would be difficult to sustain given that time had its genesis within God. (Before God created matter, there was, as Einstein's General Theory of Relativity reminds us,[31] no time.) Time therefore cannot suddenly become something bigger than God can encompass. This leads us to ask whether open theists can have both understandings of God? Can A also be non A?

There are verses in Scripture which tell us some things which God cannot do, e.g., it is impossible that God could lie (Hebrews 6:18). However, it may be argued that whilst God has the potential to lie and do evil, it is so fundamentally against God's chosen nature to do this, that we really can say that God "cannot lie." In other words, A could be non A but God chooses always to be A.[32] However, in suggesting that God is able to not know the future, we are suggesting something very much more profound than God's moral choice; we are discussing the very property of God. God cannot logically be less than he is. As such, the logical embargo on the ability of A to be non A remains a serious impediment to the possibility of God not knowing the future.

It might be suggested that God coming to us as Christ Jesus is a case where God has chosen to limit himself, a property which God might also employ in choosing not to know the future. The difficulty with this, of course, is that this property applied to only one member of the Trinity. God the Father with the Holy Spirit remained fully in control. Thus the logical difficulty, even impossibility, of God being able to be less than he is, and not know the future, remains.

What, then, can be said? Open theism brings an important emphasis to theology in highlighting the truth that God truly interacts with his creation. Whilst God is indeed far beyond that which we can now understand, God, in his greatness, chooses to be with us. The question is, do we really need the theology of open theism in order to have this understanding.

Alfred Freddoso does not think so and makes the point that, according to the traditional Christian understanding of God, "It is precisely in the person of our Lord Jesus Christ that the impassible, immutable, eternal God becomes passible, mutable, and time-bound. We Christians do not need to invent an 'open' conception of the divine nature . . . all we need to do is to contemplate Christ crucified."[33] Open theism also does well in reinforcing our understanding of the suffering that comes about as a result of moral evil.[34] However, one does not have to be an open theist to have this understanding. Many Christians have understood for some time that God made a world where evil was possible but not inevitable. God created a world with moral agents capable of rebelling and is not to blame for what human beings do with their freedom.

We therefore conclude that open theism, whilst highlighting some important truths, is not convincing in persuading us that God does not know the future. If scriptural passages exist which suggest that God is intimately and dynamically engaged with humankind, yet also knows the future, then we need a theology that allows both. Whilst open theists believe free choice to be incompatible with God's foreknowledge, it is perhaps better to understand that human free will and divine foreknowledge have to coexist. Acknowledging that it is dangerous to try and explain how God could allow both (God being so much more than we can imagine) it is nonetheless reasonable to suggest that this property of God to allow both is rooted in God's ability to stand outside of time.

Open theists such as Paul Fiddes protest at the idea that God can stand outside time. Fiddes says that if time means nothing to God, "it is hard to see how God can really be involved in our time and history."[35] However, we believe God can be intimately involved with us in time yet stand outside time if two things are taken into account. Firstly, Paul Helm reminds us that it is possible to refer to time in two ways, as A-series and as B-series. A-series time can only be understood from a point within time. Expressions such as yesterday, today, now and then are A-series expressions. God standing outside time could not be contained within such an understanding of time, as such, these concepts risk being meaningless to God. However, a B-series of time is purely an understanding of sequence, e.g., knowing that Caesar Augustus lived before Napoleon Bonaparte. God with a B-series view of time would know the sequence of all historical events and the point in history at which we stand, and so would be able to understand our temporal lot.[36]

Whilst God having a B-series view of time may explain how God can appreciate the sequence of events in our lives, it does rather suggest that it may be difficult for God to share our sense of immediacy in the present unless a second factor is understood. It is this: God's knowledge of our future does not disqualify him from understanding our feelings in the present any more than a father's knowledge of what is inside a gift-box under a Christmas-tree spoils his experience of the child's discovery of it. The father shares his child's experience intensely. This ability means that God can legitimately delight in our day to day decisions to involve him, yet also allow that God can look into the future and tell us what will be. As such, we can have confidence that what he has promised will come about because God has already seen it in his eternal present. We therefore have to conclude that God is not innocent in allowing suffering because of his ignorance of future events. The issue of God's providence and suffering therefore remains.

UNDERSTANDING "THE FALL"

Perhaps a better understanding of these issues can be obtained by reverting to a more orthodox theology than open theism. A clue that this may be the case is given by the feeling that exists amongst many that suffering and death are not good things, despite death and chance being necessary to allow the development of the new in a universe able to explore its fruitful potential. There is a sense of "wrongness," of things being unjust and incomplete. Polkinghorne suggests that the very fact that we wrestle with the problem of pain and suffering points to a dissatisfaction with science's cold mechanistic explanations and indicates a possibility that there is a significance which lies beyond them.[37] Do the feelings of incompleteness and injustice that arise from death and suffering point to something significant or is it merely the understandable dislike of any individual for morality and suffering? Are these feelings simply the product of evolution conferring a desire to maximize our health and longevity (for it will mean that we can procreate for a longer period of time) or is it more significant?

There are three reasons why we need to take the possibility of there being a meaning that lies beyond death and suffering seriously. The first comes from the observation that once individuals of a species have procreated, they serve no biological purpose to a species' existence other than to fulfill the brief but important role of helping to nurture the younger generation in a way that maximizes their chances of survival. This being the case, it seems curious that evolution has not come to our aid by selecting a behavior pattern within us that makes us happy to die once we have procreated and done what we can to ensure the survival of the next generation.

Secondly, the existence of the anthropic principle and the evidence of cosmic order suggests a meaning that lies beyond science's empiricism.

Thirdly, humankind's experience of God is too compelling to be dismissed lightly.

Is there, then, a theology that says to us that we are right to consider suffering and death as bad or imperfect for reasons other than the obvious fact that they are physically and emotionally unpleasant? I believe there is. It is orthodox Christian theology. According to orthodox Christian theology, death and suffering came about as a consequence of humankind choosing to live in an autonomous way outside the lordship of God. This truth is powerfully illustrated by the theologically illustrative story of Adam and Eve and their "fall" from God's perfect provision for them (an idyllic garden existence) as a result of them choosing not to live according to God's ways. Suffering, the story teaches, was a consequence of disobedience (Genesis 3:16–19), and death would ensure that humankind would not be trapped eternally in an imperfect state, corrupted by evil (Genesis 3:19, 22).

Theology Completes Science 115

One who expresses this orthodox understanding well is the German philosophical theologian Paul Tillich (1886–1965). Tillich says that the symbol of "the fall" is a decisive part of the Christian tradition. The story is a symbol that goes beyond Adam's fall and has universal anthropological significance.[38] He says that the possibility of the fall is grounded in the fact that humanity alone possessed the finite freedom to deny their essential nature and destroy their own humanity. It does this by choosing to sin. Tillich describes sin as estrangement from God brought about by unbelief. It is characterized by 1) lack of faith, 2) hubris (pride, i.e., humans making themselves existentially the center of their own selves rather than being centered on God), and 3) concupiscence (the unbounded striving after knowledge, sex, and power).[39] Tillich firmly believes that the fall of human beings has cosmic significance.[40] Nature is included in the fall because, he believes, one cannot separate human beings from nature. They participate in each other.[41]

If this is true, it means that a full understanding of suffering and death (beyond them being mechanisms which allow a fruitful universe) will not be possible unless we understand that, useful as they are, they are flawed mechanisms. They represent a departure from God's will. As such, we are right in considering them, at least in part, as bad. The Genesis story teaches us that God's creation was good in its initial intention. God describes it as good, (Genesis 1:4, 10, 12, 18, 21, 25, 31). However, in giving humankind freewill to choose between good and evil, evil was allowed the chance to hijack God's best plan for creation. The consequence of this was suffering and death, which not only affected humankind but all of creation. Creation therefore now "groans" as a woman painfully halted in childbirth (the birth of God's best will) and is now, as the Bible puts it, in "bondage to decay" (Romans 8:18–23).[42]

The beauty of this classical understanding is that it ties together three threads. First, it allows room for the scientific necessity of death and suffering; secondly, it satisfies the deep feeling within us that suffering and death, whilst necessary, are not fully "good"; and thirdly, it reflects divine revelation in the biblical witness.

What can we now say to Charles Darwin who found it so hard to believe in a loving God in the face of so much suffering? It is not enough to say to him that he is right to be appalled at suffering for it represents a flawed system, a departure from God's best will. That alone would not convince anyone of God's beneficence. Three further issues need to be addressed. Firstly: is God in control? In other words, has God planned to make the imperfect universe, characterized by suffering and death, right? Secondly: does God understand the wretchedness and horror we experience in living within such an imperfect universe, i.e., are we deserted by God in our suffering? Thirdly: are we impotent and helpless in the midst of the suffering we experience now?

The Christian gospel gives answers to all three questions. Rather beautifully, it answers each question by teaching about the work of each member of the Trinity: Father, Son, and Holy Spirit.

It is the nature and work of God the Father that addresses the question: "Is God in control?" and: "Will God have the last word over suffering and death?" The Bible teaches that God the Father has a plan to rescue creation back to himself. It was this plan that Jesus the Son was engaged to carry out during his ministry on earth. Jesus repeatedly said that his purpose was to do the will of his Father (Matthew 26:39; John 6:38). The actions of the Son in fulfilling the will of the Father made it plain that the Father was not content to let sin, suffering and death go unchallenged. The Father has made it clear that he will have the last word when he finally establishes his kingdom in all its fullness. When Jesus was asked by his disciples when this would be, Jesus replied, "No one knows about that day or hour, not even the angels in heaven, nor the Son, but only the Father" (Matthew 24:36).

God the Father is also the parent who allows a world of risk to provide the necessary backdrop for us to act out our moral choices. Whilst not wishing to sanitize or justify pain, there are some things that are only taught through suffering. The Father therefore allows some pain to help us mature (2 Corinthians 1:8–9; James 1:2–4; 1 Peter 1:6–7). The Christian leader and author, Rick Warren says, "God is far more concerned with our character than he is with our comfort. His plan is to perfect us, not to pamper us. For this reason he allows all kinds of character-building circumstances: conflict, disappointment, difficulty, temptation, times of dryness and delays."[43]

As vile and evil as any event of suffering may be, it will never be allowed to overcome the Father's authority entirely. God always insists in being present in the agony of suffering, not only to strengthen and comfort us in it by his Spirit, but also to extract from the situation some reform, some improved character and, above all, hope. Thus, whilst God the Father may not cause the suffering, he can use it.[44] Christians are therefore called to be a people who do not let suffering have the last word. They are called to be a people who will not be totally overcome by it. This is why the Bible teaches us to give God thanks "in" all things rather than "for" all things (1 Thessalonians 5:18).

The Father represents the sovereignty of God. He is the one who has the plans for the universe in his hands and who guarantees its ending. Because God the Father hates evil, suffering, and injustice even more than we do, he will not tolerate the existing imperfect order of things forever but has set a time when this will be replaced by a new order that is uncorrupted by sin, death, and suffering. The sovereignty of the Father means that this future is guaranteed, a future in which every tear will be wiped dry (Revelation 21:1–4). God the Father shows that God is in control and will make all things right in the end.

However, it is poor comfort to know that God has the ultimate end in hand when we are caught up in the savagery and pain of existence now. Not many people, these days, are impressed by the thought of "pie in the sky when you die." What assurance do we have that God understands what this is like and what assurance do we have that God has not deserted us in our suffering?

The Son, as God incarnate, is God's answer to those who, in their suffering, rage against God's apparent uncaring immutability. Those who have raged in such a way include Karl Marx, Albert Camus, and the critical theorists Theodor Adorno and Max Horkheimer.[45] Scholars have termed the unbelief that arises out of a deep sense of the suffering and evil of the world "protest atheism."[46] Protest atheists insist that even if there were a God, the misery which is the lot of so many people would make him or her reject God because "the divine is responsible for and does nothing to transform the human condition."[47] They ask how anyone can be expected to believe in a just, omnipotent God who is unmoved by suffering. Because Auschwitz took place in full view of God, God failed the test. Camus dramatizes the stance of protest atheism in his work The Plague in which his character, Dr. Rieux, watches the torturous death of a child and says, "Until my dying day I shall refuse to love a scheme of things in which children are put to torture."[48]

The revelation of God the Son shows that God is not above us in our misery but alongside us in our darkness, not only sharing our pain but also suffering for us (Hebrews 2:18; 4:15). God is therefore no distant uninvolved God. He came to live with us, being born a suspected illegitimate child and growing up to have no home of his own. We learn that he wept, got tired, was betrayed by friends and was executed in one of the most humiliating and painful ways devised by humankind. These facts shatter any preconception about an immutable uncaring God and show the extent to which God identifies with us. As C. S. Lewis says, the incarnation of God as Jesus "leaves all previous ideas about God in ruins."[49] The theologian, Jürgen Moltmann, is helpful in reminding us that the ability to suffer is connected to the ability to love. Those who love are vulnerable. Nowhere is this seen more clearly than at the cross which he describes as "the event of God's love." God, because of his love, is vulnerable to our suffering.[50]

Jesus the Son not only assures us in our suffering that God understands and suffers with us but also the very ministry of Jesus points to the eventual overthrow of suffering. Jesus was vitally concerned with breaking people free from all that oppressed them and expressed his intention of doing this right at the start of his ministry (Luke 4:17–21). Whenever Jesus saw suffering and sickness, he treated it as an implacable enemy to be overcome (Matthew 8:16–17; Luke 4:12–21).[51] In Jesus' healings, we see God reaching into the future kingdom and applying its principles to the present moment. This should not only give us great confidence in God's attitude to our suffering but also give us confidence in the nature of God's future kingdom.

God may have identified with us in our suffering as Jesus, but is our only response to suffering an expectation that we simply wait resignedly for God's future kingdom? Is God simply a compassionate observer watching our impotence in the face of suffering? Waite Willis (Professor of Religion at Florida Southern College) is scornful of any theism that attempts to explain suffering simply by pointing to a higher purpose. He suggests that it is only by returning to a trinitarian understanding of God that we can answer the challenge of the protest atheist. "Trinitarian theology does not give a facile response to the problem of suffering, but on the contrary makes it possible to be as rigorous in an unwillingness to accept human pain as protest atheism."[52]

He points out that Jesus came in history to a socio-political context bringing concrete liberation, not just a projected future hope. This work of Jesus continues today through the work of God's Spirit in the church. The third and final factor that helps answer the challenge of suffering is therefore God's empowering presence in the form of the Holy Spirit. God's Spirit does not simply empower us to endure suffering[53] but, most significantly, compels Christians to address suffering in a practical way whenever they come across it.

A number of Christian traditions have particularly focused on practical ministry to those in need. It has, for example, been an important feature in the ministry of those engaged in Liberation Theology. The Liberation theologian, Matthew Lamb is one who does not believe Christians are called to apathetic resignation in the face of suffering. Rather, he suggests Christians are called to "agapic praxis," i.e., they are called by God to engage in acts of liberation on behalf of the poor and the powerless. The appropriate act of liberation is defined after reflection on what particular action best reflects God's standard of self-transcending love. He goes on to suggest that a faith that compels agapic praxis is the only way to address suffering given the fact that humankind has failed so lamentably to address it without such a faith.[54] Lamb's liberation theology highlights the necessity for faith to be expressed in practical acts of love[55] and it is the Holy Spirit of God that sees to it that Christians are equipped to do so.

The Pentecostal theologian, Gordon Fee, reminds us that, for the apostle Paul, the Holy Spirit was not merely an impersonal force, influence or power. The Spirit was none other than the fulfillment of the promise that God himself would once again be present with his people.[56] Paul believed that the gift of "the promised Holy Spirit" (Ephesians 1:13) was certain evidence that the future had already been set in motion. He expected visible demonstrations of God's power through the Spirit to be manifested in the church's ministry even in the midst of weakness. For Paul, it was not simply that the present was all weakness and the future all glory but that the future had truly broken into the present, as verified by the gift of the Spirit.[57] We are therefore called to embrace the Spirit of God so we can minister in the power of God. Whilst it is not appropriate for Christians to do this in a triumphalist way (because the benefits of God's coming kingdom are not yet fully realized) the Holy Spirit's power should nonetheless still be evident in equipping Christians for ministry and empowering them to address suffering wherever it is found.

Whilst our understanding of the vexing issue of suffering will always be incomplete, Christianity nonetheless gives a comprehensive and satisfying metaphysical framework for understanding it. Christianity allows that death permits the universe to explore its fruitful potential, but it also agrees with the emotional response of most humans that death and suffering are not "good" things but reflect a system that is not right. Christianity explains this imperfection as being the result of humankind's rebellion against God, something which has impacted all of creation and all of time (indicated by the fact that suffering has not been restricted to the brief time of humankind's existence). Sin is able to do this because it is an affront to God who stands outside time.

Not all theologians are willing to accept that the presence of imperfection is due to humankind's initial rebellion. For example, Polkinghorne can not believe with Augustine that humankind's abuse of freewill and decision to sin has had cosmic consequences for all of creation.[58] He would rather explain physical evil as the inevitable consequence of a world exploring its own potentiality through the shifting operations of happen-stance. He understands the initial goodness of creation to be fruitful potentiality rather than initial perfection.[59] This understanding is consistent with Polkinghorne's insistence on scientific congruency. However, this congruency must be more than theology simply redrawing the boundaries of science.

A difficulty with Polkinghorne's understanding is that it is now widely understood that time began with the big bang. By holding God a prisoner in time by saying that God does not know the future, Polkinghorne does not adequately explain what God was doing before time began. The theologian Alan Padgett is right when he suggests that a picture of God who is everlasting within time is not compatible with modern physics that teaches that time is a created thing.[60]

An inadequate theology of the fall (Adam's fall, i.e., human sin) and its impact on creation as well as humankind, will inevitably result in a more impersonal fatalistic understanding of God. It results in God simply being a distant deity who imbues the universe with generators of random novelty and creativity which produce outcomes even God can not predict. In other words, science's God simply rolls the dice. However, if the "fall" (and its impact on creation) is understood, God's holiness is understood, and if God's holiness is understood, God's judgment on humankind and on nature is understood. Some examples of the impact of evil on nature are seen in natural catastrophes, the existence of which points to the need for all of humankind to call on God in repentance (Luke 13:1–5). Notwithstanding the positive side of pain, God's judgment on sin, suffering, and death means it is also possible to name physical suffering as evil, something that is fundamentally the result of godlessness. Polkinghorne seems shy of doing this although he does say that the fall has a moral significance that lies deeper than the recognition of this world's transience.[61]

According to Polkinghorne, happen-stance and risk are both necessary to allow burgeoning fruitfulness and diversity in the universe. However, we suggest that evil is more systemic and prevalent than Polkinghorne's fruitful chance requires.[62] He fails to account for gratuitous evil which seems to have little to do with being the necessary cost of allowing cosmic possibilities. There seems no scientific reason why evil is so pervasive. For some, this points to the non-existence of

God or, if he does exist, God's impotence or callous neglect. For headway to be made in understanding the existence of evil in the cosmos, we have to take more seriously the sinful, imperfect nature of creation that awaits God's redemption. Only when this is factored in will we understand that creation is fundamentally flawed because of evil (Genesis 3).

In making this suggestion, I am doing more than appealing to a few verses in Genesis 3 and Romans 8 that refer to the "fall" of humankind. The concept of the fall reflects the main theme of the whole Bible, which is God rescuing humankind back from the consequences of sin to himself. Whilst the Bible features humankind as the main object of God's action in this drama, the concept of human sin also impacting all of creation is a consistent one in Scripture. It exists as theology presented in story form in Genesis 3:17–19. It was also an understanding that was consistently taught in Old Testament Jewish history. Writers of the Old Testament wrote that, whenever people sinned against God, it resulted in their land being unproductive. As such, sin defiled the land (Isaiah.24:4–6; Jeremiah 2:7). "Defiling a land" was therefore more than a comment on the morality of the people, it literally meant good land being laid waste (Psalm 107:33–34; Jeremiah 9:12–13; Hosea 4:1–3). Whilst such Old Testament prophecies have echoes of ancient suzerainty treaties in which victorious nations sought to encourage the faithfulness of vassal states by invoking blessings or curses on them, we should hesitate to dismiss such verses simply as culturally anachronistic literary devices. Testimony is being given, even today, that links between Christian faithfulness and the productivity of a land still exist.[63] In other words, they do seem to point to an underlying principle.

This is not to suggest that we retreat to the theologically simplistic notion that good things happen to good people and bad things to bad people. It is much more complex than that. What is being suggested is that suffering is, at its most fundamental level, an imperfection in the universe brought about by our departure from God's lordship. As humankind has only been present in the universe for a brief time, the spiritual consequences of our sin against God (for whom time is no barrier) is that it may impact all of creation across time.

In conclusion, although the biblical concept of the fall as an explanation for death and suffering might appear to some as a culturally quaint, fundamentalist position, nonetheless, it does seem to present fewer problems than purely scientific explanations. As such, its principles deserve to be taken more seriously. Its teaching that humankind's rebellion against God has impacted all of creation makes sense of death and suffering. It also points to the hope we have that God is rescuing us back to himself through Jesus and is giving us an invitation to share in his new creation when all will be made new (John 10:14–16; 14:1–4).

6

Conclusion

> *Science and religion cannot be confined to their separate compartments and ignore each other. They are each concerned with truth and there cannot be multiple truths which are completely unconnected with each other.*
>
> —Fraser Watts, Science Meets Faith, p.13.

THE CHURCH HAS A major PR challenge. It needs to address the perception that Christianity lacks scientific credibility. The South Australian survey on science and faith showed that 70 percent of those surveyed believe that Christianity has generally been antagonistic towards science throughout history. Not only that, but 84 percent believed that science continues to discredit the Christian faith to some degree. The concern of the religious historian John Stenhouse would seem to be well founded. He wrote:

> Why in the modern West is science so widely perceived to suggest the non-existence of God, especially of the Christian God? This is a crucial question, because unless scientism – that is, the scientific imperialism which claims there is no reality beyond science and the natural – can be effectively challenged, no form of theology, natural or revealed, can begin to get off the ground. An historical understanding and critique of scientism is thus a fundamental task for Christian apologetics.[1]

It is to this end that this book is written.

Whilst many Christian theologians are encouraged by the new wave of cooperation and dialogue between scientists and theologians in the last 30 years, there is little evidence that knowledge of this dialogue has reached those not immediately involved with it. The recent level of cooperation between science and faith still seems to be overwhelmed by media reports of emotive battles between biblical literalists (who are often portrayed as representing the Christian community) and the scientific community. Conrad Hyers writes, "Many scientists and intellectuals have simply taken the literalists at their word and rejected biblical materials as being superseded or contradicted by modern science . . . Intellectual integrity demands it."[2]

When a DVD on Intelligent Design, entitled "Unlocking the Mystery of Life"[3] was sent to all schools in Australia in 2006, it provoked a sharp reaction in the media. The DVD suggests that whilst Darwinian evolution works well at a limited scale, it fails to account for the full complexity we see in life. This complexity is better explained by saying it is the result of intelligent design. The DVD features many of the leaders of the Intelligent Design movement including Phillip Johnson, Jonathan Wells, Paul Nelson, Steve Meyer (who helped write the script) and William Dembski. Many of these scientists are associated with the Discovery Institute in America, an institution which has played a key role in popularizing the concept of Intelligent Design.

A move to introduce Intelligent Design to schools in America also provoked a sharp reaction in the media from many in the scientific community. The American archaeologist R. Joe Brandon organized a four-day on-line campaign. He circulated a petition between September 28th and October 1st, 2006 which gave scientists the opportunity to publicly state that Intelligent Design should not be taught in public schools within the science curriculum.[4] The petition resulted in an impressive 7,733 signatories, more than half of whom were scientists with PhDs. Evidently, many people were suspicious that the initiatives of the Discovery Institute were a sneaky way of smuggling Christian fundamentalism into mainstream education. Pre-enlightenment religion was suspected of making a comeback and religious dogma was seen to be threatening the intellectual integrity of our children's school curriculum.

In a widely publicized trial, eleven parents of Dover Area School (Pennsylvania, USA) brought a legal case against the school board for allowing the teaching of Intelligent Design as an option alongside evolution to explain biological complexity.[5] On the 20th September, 2005, the court ruled against the school board and against the validity of Intelligent Design.

A key witness for the plaintiffs was Kenneth Miller, professor of biology at Brown University (Providence, Rhode Island) and author of the book Finding Darwin's God. During the trial, Miller described his book as an attempt to explain why the scientific community found evolution to be such a useful and compelling scientific explanation. Miller, a Roman Catholic, explained that his book sought to explain how anyone following any of the great Abrahamic religions could appreciate evolution in the context of their faith.

The biologist Michael Behe, biochemist at Lehigh University (Bethlehem, Pennsylvania) and author of Darwin's Black Box, appeared on behalf of the defense Behe claimed that there are some biological systems, such as the flagellum (a whip-like hair that propels some single celled bacteria through a liquid medium), which are "irreducibly complex." He argued that the flagellum is an integrated whole. It is made up of forty component parts which build the rotor, stator, U joint, drive shaft and propeller of this molecular machine. Thirty of these forty component parts do not seem to exist in any other cellular structures. As all forty pieces are necessary for the flagellum to operate, it is difficult to imagine how the flagellum could have evolved through small modifications which added new parts over time. The component parts would confer no biological advantage until they all existed together and were constructed in a very specific way to form this particular molecular machine. The bacterial flagellum is therefore irreducibly complex and shows evidence of intelligent design.

Miller countered Behe's argument by saying that the bacterial flagellum is not irreducibly complex. Nature is filled with examples of precursors to the flagellum that are "missing a part" and are yet fully functional.[6]

On current evidence, Behe's argument is not compelling. Nature shows little evidence of leaps in organizational structure within living organisms which don't have more primitive precursors. Life really is remarkably integrated.

Whilst this is so, the building of the highly complex protein molecules which are the building blocks for the genetic mechanisms of living organisms is more of a mystery. Evolution requires a self-replicating system, and complex protein molecules are not independently existing, self-replicating systems able to vary in ways that confer an evolutionary advantage to themselves. Their existence therefore remains a puzzle. As such, it is entirely legitimate to ask where this drive towards increasingly organized molecular structures comes from. Universal ground rules seem to exist that allow for the possibility of increasingly complex life forms. Why is this so? This is the level at which Intelligent Design can perhaps legitimately be considered.

It is very much to be regretted that the question of Intelligent Design has been sensationalized in the media with claims that it will teach our children that the Earth was built by God in six 24 hour days. Ideally, Intelligent Design should stimulate intelligent debate about the origins of the ordered universe we live in. It should not be a signal to return to the trench warfare that existed between science and faith in the nineteenth century. The fierce reaction to Intelligent Design shown by some humanists should not be allowed to gag discussion any more than the sixteenth century Catholic Church should have been allowed to gag discussions about science. Education is all about allowing inquiry and exploring the edges of knowledge. This inquiry must not be prevented by ideologically driven humanists on the left, or hijacked by Biblical literalists on the right.

It is scientifically reasonable to ask why the universe is so remarkably suited to allow intelligent life to develop on at least one planet. There are infinite ways our universe could have been chaotic but ours is not. It runs according to ordered, understandable laws which have a mathematical beauty. To dismiss this by saying that ours is probably a chance existence from an infinite number of possibilities is a manifestly inadequate response to the highly unlikely, ordered reality that actually exists.

Claims that our universe is remarkable have been dismissed by some who say that such assertions are akin to seeing a number plate on a car whilst traveling to work and then explaining after the event, "Who would have thought I'd see that particular number plate today? The odds against me seeing that particular number plate are enormous." Remarking on something after the event in this way is, of course, ridiculous: but this is not a fair analogy. It would make better sense, although not altogether good sense, to say, "Today I saw a number plate on a car composed of thousands of figures which were arranged in the code necessary for building molecules to support the life form *Homo sapiens*." In other words, it is not just the fact of our existence but the manner of our existence that is significant: and this, quite rightly, demands some sort of explanation. As such, it is scientifically reasonable to wonder why the extraordinarily complex protein molecules that carry the codes of a specific life form developed. It cannot be the result of evolution as it is commonly understood, as evolution can only work at the level of self-replicating organisms. The English Physicist and committed atheist Fred Hoyle made the point that the probability of making a single functioning protein by a chance combination of amino acids was as likely as a solar system full of blind men solving Rubik's cube simultaneously.[7]

Logic, rather than ideology, must therefore allow scientists to posit the possibility of Intelligent Design as far as it applies to the ordered fabric of the universe—if that order is found to be both widespread and understandable. However, as has been previously stressed, care needs to be taken that we do not lazily ascribe to God all those things we do not understand in science. This is because science has a habit of gradually discovering how things work, causing the need to invoke God to continually be in retreat.

The Christian faith is scientifically reasonable. Many Christians believe the Genesis accounts of creation are timeless stories designed to tell us theology's "who and why" rather than science's "how and when." Many Christians also accept that evolution is a remarkably good and well attested theory that explains how the diversity of living forms came to be. However, evolution cannot explain the order we see at a cosmic level or the order that we see at a molecular level.

It must be remembered that over 70 percent of the population of Australia believe in some sort of God. This means that most Australians believe that creation is a purposeful act, i.e., intelligently designed, to some degree. It is a position shared by Charles Darwin, Albert Einstein, Paul Davies, and Stephen Hawking. Their quotes bear repeating:

> I have never been an atheist in the sense of denying the existence of God. (Charles Darwin)[8]

> Science without religion is lame, religion without science is blind. (Albert Einstein)[9]

> I belong to a group of scientists who do not subscribe to a conventional religion but nevertheless deny that the universe is a purposeless accident. Through my scientific work I have come to believe more and more strongly that the universe is put together with an ingenuity so astonishing that I cannot accept it merely as brute fact. (Paul Davies)[10]

> The odds against a universe like ours emerging out of something like the Big Bang are enormous. I think there are clearly religious implications. (Stephen Hawking)[11]

It would be unwise for anyone to consign the above scientists to the lunatic asylum reserved for religious fundamentalists. The concept of Intelligent Design as it applies to the ordered nature of the universe, deserves serious debate—a debate that will inevitably touch on the core issues of our identity and meaning.

AN INVITATION TO A DUET

Science and theology are not inherently antagonistic toward each other but are compatible and can enrich each other. Science can provide theology with an understanding of physical reality, so supplying theology with the physical context within which it can explore issues of meaning and faith. Science can also constrain the Christian church from making poorly grounded theological claims based on speculation, institutional self-interest, ignorance or a simplistic understanding of biblical authority.

For its part, Christian theology can help constrain scientists from passing off speculation as unassailable science and can help rescue science from errors that result from atheistic presuppositions. Theology can also help break science out of its empiricist prison so it can be informed by other ways of knowing that more fully reflect our total experience of reality. After all, to describe a kiss simply as the contraction of cheek and lip muscles in a mutual exchange of carbon-dioxide, saliva and micro-organisms is probably an inadequate description of its full meaning, something your sweetheart would soon insist you understood!

Not only can theology introduce other ways of knowing but it can also help ensure that what is popularly believed has a solid basis in fact. Part of this will involve presenting an accurate overview of the relationship between science and Christianity through history.

It seems that the failings of the institutional church regarding Galileo and Darwin have proved more formative of opinion than the fact that science has flourished in cultures with a Christian heritage. I have sought to bring a more balanced understanding by making it clear that science and Christianity are not growing increasingly apart but have had a relationship in which the two disciplines have continually moved together and apart through history. Moreover, this relationship between the two disciplines is one that is currently characterized by very significant levels of dialogue and cooperation.

Science is not antagonistic to faith but helps us understand that creation is infused with order, which, although it does not compel faith, should at least point to the possibility of the existence of God (Romans 1:20). However, the notion that the extraordinary order of the universe is supportive of the Christian concept of God is challenged by people who point out the reality of suffering, chance and chaos that exists in the natural world.

Science tells us that random events, death and competition between organisms are necessary factors required in order to allow the generation of new developments within a universe that seems so conducive to allowing increasing diversity. However, science struggles to go any further. It merely leaves us with a God who is either impotent in his ability to exert total control, or who chooses not to exert total control because he is unmoved by our suffering and is careless of which species evolve.

As we have seen, some scientists have attempted to explain suffering by suggesting that God does not know the future but has imbued the universe with the ability to generate authentic novelty that even he has not predicted. The cost of having such a fruitful universe able to invent itself is evolutionary blind alleys, suffering, and death. The possibility of God not knowing the future has also been suggested by theologians. They see biblical reasons for believing that God does not know the future and has chosen not to know it so that he can have an authentic relationship with humankind in time. Because God does not know the future, he is not culpable for the suffering we cause by choosing not to live in partnership with God.

Whilst there is some truth in God choosing to limit the full expression of his omnipotence now in order to allow us free-will, the idea that God does not know the future poses more problems than it solves. It presents logical difficulties and disagrees with many biblical texts which testify to God's omnipotence. Little progress will be made in resolving the conundrum of suffering unless orthodox Christian theology is allowed to make more of a contribution to the debate.

Theology can help our search for meaning because it can factor in God's self-revelation, particularly as Christ Jesus. It allows Christology to introduce the personal element of God to what would otherwise be a sterile, impersonal, scientific view of a divine being who is engaged in cosmic experimentation, uncommitted to the existence of humankind. As such, cosmology is incomplete without Christology. Without an understanding of Christ, science has no manger to lie in. It is God's bestowal of love and self-revelation in Christ that underwrites our worth and gives meaning to our existence. An understanding of Christ's mission will also help us to understand the issues of purpose, suffering, evil, and hope.

It is therefore important for science to dialogue with theology. Both our spiritual experiences of God in history (distilled as theology) and our experiences of God's handiwork in nature (distilled as science) need to be acknowledged if we are to talk of the complete human experience of God. This is why there should be consonance between the disciplines of science and theology.

However, introducing the Christian understanding of God who reaches out to us in love highlights rather than solves the issue of suffering. The issue becomes even more of a conundrum in that suffering exists in the face of a caring, all-powerful God. Christianity gives three perspectives that help make sense of this. Firstly, it recognizes that life without pain is neither possible nor desirable in that some pain is necessary to teach us and help us mature. Secondly, Christianity takes the reality of evil seriously and understands that some suffering arises through our poor moral choices. God, in seeking our authentic, freely given love, gives us freedom to choose his lordship or to reject it. The high price God was prepared to pay for our freely given love was to allow us to live with the consequences of the actions we choose (epitomized by the obscenity of Auschwitz).

I have also offered a third perspective that seeks to make sense of suffering caused by the inherent dangers of living in the natural world, e.g., the suffering that is caused by the non-moral agencies of earthquakes and volcanoes, etc. The suggestion is that we take the theology of "the fall" seriously and agree with the Apostle Paul who used it to explain, not only the suffering caused by the moral choices of humankind, but also the suffering caused in nature by the natural world. Paul's suggestion was that all of creation, across time and space, became spoilt by the sin of humankind. In other words, the universe is a good thing spoilt. This is why we can both marvel at its beauty and its order, yet grieve over the harsh realities of the suffering which occurs within it.

By saying that God created and purposed humankind with whom he seeks to have a loving friendship, Christianity is making a cosmic claim. Christians therefore cannot separate science from theology. Even though the relationship between the two disciplines is not always straightforward, they have discovered that Christian theology completes and augments the convictions that come from scientific observation. As such, there are solid grounds for saying that theology offers an understanding that gives science its ground of meaning. As such, science and theology are not inherently antagonistic toward each other but are compatible and can enrich each other.

Christians believe that science helps introduces us to the possibility of God. According to the teaching of Jesus, this God seeks our love and has paid a huge price to secure it. Nowhere else will you see an invitation to a relationship that is as large as the cosmos, as intimate as a child in a manger or as committed as a man on a cross.

Endnotes

INTRODUCTION

1. J. Le Conte, *Religion and Science* (New York: D. Appleton and Company, 1902), 11.
2. A survey conducted on the 18th June, 2001 of all the books in the science section of the largest Christian bookshop in Adelaide, Koorong Books, indicated that of the 50 books that discussed evolution, 34 were anti-evolution, i.e., were against conventional science.
3. This understanding is fueled by books such as S. M. Huse, *The Collapse of Evolution*, 3rd edition, (Grand Rapids, MI: Baker Book House, 1998) and H. M. Morris, *The Twilight of Evolution*, 2nd edition, (North Santee, CA: Institute for Creation Research, 1998).
4. P. Kaldor and R. Powell, *Views from the Pews*, National Church Life Survey (Adelaide: Openbook Publishers, 1995), 68. Whilst half of current churchgoers are content to hold non-scientific beliefs, it will be seen that educated non-church attenders to whom this apologetic is directed are not.
5. 62 percent of those aged between 15–19 were creationist compared with 43 percent of those over the age of 70 (*Views from the Pews*, 68–69). Note: the Catholic Church was not included in this survey.
6. Reported by John Rennie, in: J. Rennie, "15 Answers to Creationist Nonsense," pages 62–69 in *Scientific American*, 287 (July 2002): 65.
7. 60 percent of mathematicians and 55 percent of physical and life scientists were religious compared with 29 percent of anthropologists and 33 percent of psychologists, see: R. Stark and R. Finke, *Acts of Faith: Explaining the Human Side of Religion* (Berkeley, CA: University of California Press, 2000), 53.
8. E. J. Larson, and L. Witham, "Scientists are still keeping the faith," *Nature*, 386, (1997) 435–36. Larson and Witham followed this survey up with another in 1998 which focused on more eminent scientists (members of the National Academy of Sciences). They discovered that amongst these leading scientists, only 7 percent expressed belief in God. See: E. J. Larson, and L. Witham, "Leading scientists still reject God," *Nature*, 394, (1998): 313.
9. Stark and Finke, *Acts of Faith*, 73.
10. R. J. Russell, "How the Heaven's Have Changed," pages 3–10 in *CTNS Bulletin* 19, (Berkeley, CA), 4. Robert Russell, physicist and theologian, is Director of The Center for Theology and the Natural Sciences, Berkeley, CA.
11. A television program about the spiritual beliefs of British people was broadcast in nine episodes in June and July, 2000 on BBC TV. The program called, "Soul of Britain," (presented by Michael Buerk) was based on a survey of beliefs and

attitudes commissioned by the BBC and conducted by Opinion Research Business on a representative sample of 1000 people in Britain.
12. N. J. Hawkes, An apology for the scientific credibility of faith, (DMin Thesis, Australian College of Theology, 2004), 6–12.
13. Non-church attenders were classed as those who would not normally attend a Christian church more than once a month.

CHAPTER 1

The Changing Relationship Between Science and Christianity

1. Charles Darwin, in a letter first published in 1887 by his son Francis Darwin: (F. Darwin [ed.], *The Life and Letters of Charles Darwi*n 2 vols, [London, 1887, Vol 1], 304). These volumes were later published in the United States of America in 1898. Volume 1 can be viewed on: www.pages.britishlibrary,net/charles.darwin/texts/letters/letters1_fml.
2. N. Hawkes, *An Apology for the Scientific Credibility of Faith*, DMin Thesis, (Sydney: Australian College of Theology, 2004), 18–19.
3. Richard Dawkins is a prolific author but his vehemently atheistic stance particularly became public with the publication of *The Selfish Gene* (Oxford: Oxford University Press, 1976) and *The Blind Watchmaker: Why the Evidence of Evolution reveals a Universe without Design.* (New York: W.W. Norton, 1986).
4. J. Polkinghorne, *Quarks, Chaos and Christianity* (London: Triangle, SPCK, 1994), 17–18. For information on the attitude of ancient Greeks to work, see: C. Mosse, *The Ancient World at Work*, (London: Chatto & Windus, 1969), 27–28.
5. Augustine, *De Genesi ad litteram*, II.9, I.21, trans E. McMullin, "How Should Cosmology Relate to Theology?" pages 17–57 in A. R. Peacocke, (ed.) *The Sciences and Theology in the Twentieth Century*, (London: Oriel Press, 1981),19.
6. Cited by E. McMullin, "How Should Cosmology Relate to Theology?" 20–21.
7. Augustine, *Confessions* XI.14, trans R. S. Pine-Coffin, (London: Penguin, 1961), 263. (In older English but easily accessible at: www.ccel.org/paper.cgi?file=a/augustine/confessions) Augustine treated the nature of time more extensively in his *City of God* trans. H. Bettenson, (Harmondsworth: *Penguin Books*, 1972) Book XI, chapters 4–6.
8. Ernan McMullin describes this debate as being "the most serious intellectual crisis the church had faced in almost a thousand years" (McMullin, "How Should Cosmology Relate to Theology?" 29).
9. It is now widely understood that time began with the big bang, see: Paul Davies (in conversation with Phillip Adams) *The Big Questions* (Melbourne: Penguin Books Australia, 1996), 11.
10. This law indicates that the cosmos is inexorably moving towards a cessation of material processes.
11. Fred Hoyle, The Nature of the Universe, (Oxford: Blackwell, 1950).
12. Augustine, *De Genesi ad litteram*, V.5, V.23, in: J. H. Taylor (trans.), *The Literal Meaning of Genesis*, 2 vols. (No.41 & 42), Ancient Christian Writers series, No. 41, (New York: Newman Press, 1982, Vol.1), 153–56, 159–60.

13. Augustine, *De Genesi ad litteram*, I.18.37, I.20.40, in: J. H. Taylor (trans.), *The Literal Meaning of Genesis*, Vol.1, 41. Augustine warned, for example that "days" in the Genesis account could not be taken literally since the sun was not created until the fourth day.
14. Thomas Aquinas, *Summa Theologica* First part, Question 2, Article 3. (see: www.newadvent.org/summa/100203.htm).
15. N. Emerton, "Arguments for the existence of God from nature and science," pages 72–86 in *Science and Theology: Questions at the Interface*, M. Rae, H. Regan and J. Stenhouse (eds.) (Edinburgh: T&T Clark, 1994), 74.
16. Nicholas Copernicus was a Polish scholar, who wrote: *de revolutionibus orbitum coelestium* (on the revolutions of the heavenly bodies) in May 1543, in which he said that the earth rotated on its own axis whilst circling around the sun. In doing this, Copernicus further advanced the theory first postulated by the Greek astronomer Aristarchus of Samos (about 270 BC) that the earth revolved around the sun. Whilst Copernicus' work was a breakthrough in understanding, it did not explain all observations. It wasn't until Johannes Kepler (1571–1630) modified Copernicus' theory to allow for elliptical orbits and discovered that the square of the time of orbit of the planets was proportional to the cube of their distance from the sun, that the anomalies were explained. See: A. E. McGrath, *Science & Religion: An introduction* (Oxford: Blackwell, 1999), 7–8.
17. R. J. Blackwell, Galileo, Bellarmine, and the Bible (Nôtre Dame, in: University of Nôtre Dame Press, 1991), 87–110.
18. Blackwell, Galileo, Bellarmine, and the Bible, 94–95.
19. B. Brundell, "Bellarmine to Foscarini on Copernicanism: A Theologian's Response," pages 375–93 in G. Freeland and A. Corones (eds.), *1543 and All That* (Great Britain: Kluwer Academic Publishers, 2000), 376–77.
20. M. Worthing, "Science and Theology—An Historical Overview," pages 5–11 in *Pacific Journal of Theology and Science* 1, (2000): 9–10.
21. Brundell, "Bellarmine to Foscarini on Copernicanism," 377–79. This same factor was to emerge in Darwin's time when freethinking views which challenged the ideas of the established church were regarded with suspicion, not simply because of their theological implications but because they gave impetus to reformist ideas that threatened the stability, culture, civility and class distinction of society—for which the Church of England had become custodian. See: A. Desmond and J. Moore, *Darwin* (London: Penguin Books, 1991), 31–34. History suggests that it was not so much Christian theology that had a problem with science so much as the often less saintly ecclesiological accretions of power and control.
22. S. Drake (tr.), *Discoveries and Opinions of Galileo* (New York: Doubleday, 1957), 194.
23. Drake (tr.), *Discoveries and Opinions of Galileo*, 185.
24. Drake (tr.), *Discoveries and Opinions of Galileo*, 188–89.
25. A. Fantoli, *Galileo: For Copernicanism and for the Church*, trans. B. V. Coyne, 2nd ed. (Vatican Observatory Foundation, 1996), 319–23.
26. A. Fantoli, *Galileo: For Copernicanism and for the Church*, 321.
27. G. Galilei, *Dialogue Concerning the Two Chief World Systems—Ptolemaic and Copernican*, trans. S. Drake, (Berkeley, CA: University of California Press, 1953).
28. Fantoli, *Galileo: For Copernicanism and for the Church*, 445–46.
29. Blackwell, *Galieo, Bellarmine and the Bible*, 53–134.
30. McGrath, *Science & Religion*, 9–10.

Endnotes

31. J. Calvin, *Commentaries: Genesis*, Vol. I, Genesis, chapter 1, verse 5, J. King (trans.), 2 vols., (Edinburgh: Calvin Translation Soc, 1843), 1.78
32. Calvin says that anyone can see God in creation but this general knowledge of God is imperfect and is not properly understood because of the inherent sinfulness of humankind. The most complete knowledge of God is only through Christian revelation. Scripture reiterates what can be known of God in nature but goes further and shows the redeeming actions of God through Jesus Christ. J. Calvin, *Institutes of the Christian Religion* ed. J. T. McNeill, trans. F. L. Battles, *The Library of Christian Classics*, Vol.XX, 2 vols, (Philadelphia: Westminster Press, 1960, Vol.1), I.1,5,14, 37–39, 50–63, 140–58.
33. McGrath, *Science & Religion*, 11. McGrath cites a paragraph added in 1543 to Calvin's preface to Olivétan's translation of the New Testament [1534] in which Calvin says that Scripture is not an astronomical, geographical or biological textbook (A. E. McGrath, *The Foundations of Dialogue in Science and Religion* [Oxford: Blackwell, 1998], 124). I have not been able to find this text. It is not present in Calvin: Commentaries, II. Preface to Olivétan's New Testament, pages 58–73 in The Library of Christian Classics Vol XXIII, Calvin: Commentaries, (London: SCM Press, 1958) despite it having additions Calvin made after 1534. For more information on the recurring motive of accommodation in Calvin's thought, see : F. L. Battles, "God was accommodating Himself to Human Capacity," *Interpretation*, 31, (1977): 19–38.
34. J. Calvin, *Commentaries: Genesis*, Vol.1, Genesis, chapter.1, verse 6, (Grand Rapids, Michigan; Baker Book House), 79.
35. J. Calvin, *Commentaries: Genesis*, Vol. 1, Genesis, chapter.1, verse 6, 80.
36. J. Calvin, *Commentaries: Genesis*, Vol. 1, Genesis, chapter 6, verse14, 256.
37. J. Calvin, *Commentaries: Genesis*, Vol. 1, Genesis, chapter 1, verse 16, J. King (trans.), 1.86.
38. J. Calvin, *Commentaries, Psalms*, Vol.4, Psalm 19, verse 4, (Grand Rapids, Michigan; Baker Book House), 313.
39. J. Calvin, *Commentaries, Psalms*, Vol.4, Psalm 19, verse 4, 315.
40. M. Luther, *Disputation Against Scholastic Theology*, (1517) discussed in: W. P. Stephens, The Theology of Huldrych Zwingli (Oxford: Clarendon Press, 1986), 235–50. and: A. E. McGrath, *Reformation Thought: An Introduction*, 2nd ed. (Oxford: Blackwell, 1993), 168–70.
41. M. Luther, *Luther's Works*, ed. & trans T. G. Tappert, 55 vols, (Philadelphia: Fortress, 1965, Vol 54), 358–59. It is perhaps ironic that the foreword to Copernicus' first book De Revolutionibus (which first presented Copernicus' ideas) was written by the Protestant Andreas Osiander. Osiander, possibly aware of the potential for controversy, was very circumspect and subdued in his presentation of Copernicus' ideas describing them only as a mathematical theory, a marvelous hypothesis that was far from certain.
42. H. Bornkamm, *Luther's World of Thought*, trans. M. H. Bertram (Saint Louis, MO: Concordia Publishing House, 1958), 177.
43. Luther, *Luther's Works*, 54: 452.
44. Translated from a Latin note written in the margin of Luther's Bible next to Romans 1:20, see: M. Luther, *Werke*, (Weimarer Ausgabe: 1927), Vol 48, 201. (Volume 48 has not yet been translated into English.)
45. Luther, Luther's *Works*, 52: 160–61.

46. Tertullian, *Contra Marcionem*, I.18. (See: ww.gnosis.org/library/ter_marc1.htm).
47. Stoic philosophy believes in one single essence, either that of nature, or of God. However, because nature and God are related, the Stoics' materialistic monism takes on pantheistic flavor, i.e., it believes that nature is God.
48. Emerton, "Arguments for the existence of God from nature and science," 65.
49. Isaac Newton was born in 1642, (the year of Galileo's death) and wrote *Principia* in which he presented equations that accurately predicted the motions of the planets and the rate at which objects fall on earth. In doing so, he vindicated the heliocentric, rotating Earth cosmology of Copernicus, Kepler, and Galileo and also showed that the same physics that worked on earth worked in the universe. See: T. Ferris, *The Whole Shebang: A State-of-the-Universe(s) Report* (London: Phoenix, 1998), 29.
50. Newton's God did little else than stop planets collapsing into the sun. From this, it was only a small step to suggest that the universe was a self-stabilizing universe which didn't need God at all.
51. G. W. Leibniz, First and Fifth Letters to Samuel Clarke in Leibniz' *Philosophical Writings*, ed. G. Parkinson, trans. M. Morris, (London: Dent, 1973), 205, 230.
52. I. Newton, *First Letter to Richard Bentley* (1692) in Newton's *Philosophy of Nature: Selections from his Writings* ed. H. S. Taylor Collins (New York: Hafner, 1953), 46.
53. J. Calvin Confessio Belgica (1561), cited in: McGrath, Science and Religion, 11.
54. J. Calvin, *Institutes of the Christian Religion*, The Library of Christian Classics, 2 vols, Vol.XX, II.2.16, 275.
55. J. Calvin, *Institutes*, Vol.XX, I.6.1, 69–71. Collins
56. Worthing, "Science and Theology—An Historical Overview," 6.
57. C. Darwin, *The Origin of Species*. (London: Penguin Books, 1985), 50.
58. F. Bacon, *The Advancement of Learning* (1605), 8 (I.1.3).
59. T. Browne, Relgio Medici (1642) ed. J. Winney (Cambridge, 1983) part I, section 16, 18–19.
60. R. Boyle, *Some Motives and Incentives to the Love of God* (1648) reprinted in 1659 (also known by the running title *Seraphick Love*, now available as: R. Boyle, *Serphic Love*, Belle Fourche, SD: Kessinger Publishing, 1992) cited in: D. L. Woodall, "The Relationship between Science and Scripture in the Thought of Collins Robert Boyle," pages 32–39 in, *Perspectives on Science and Christian Faith* 49 (1997): 32.
61. R. Boyle, *The Excellency of Theology Compared with Natural Theology* (tract, 1674), viewed at: www.neon.mems.cmu.edu/laughlin/Jub.1.pdf
62. W. Paley, *Natural Theology*, 1802, Revised and annotated edition (Edinburgh: Chambers, 1849), chapter 23, 246, cited in K. R. Miller, "Life's Grand Design." *Technology Review*, 92, (Feb./March 1994): 24–32.
63. W. Paley, *Works* ed. E. Paley, 6 vols. (London: Rivington, 1830, Vol 4), 16,34–35, cited in McGrath, *Science and Religion*, 100–1.
64. J. Brooke and G. Cantor, *Reconstructing Nature: The Engagement of Science and Religion*, (Edinburgh: T&T Clark, 1988), 163.
65. The philosopher, Ernan McMullin, suggests that the term "creationist" for proponents of creation science is "both unfortunate and confusing, since nearly all Christians believe in God as Creator, but relatively few adopt the literalist reading of the first chapters of Genesis that under-girds creation science." See: E. McMullin, "Life and Intelligence Far from Earth: Formulating Theological Issues," pages 151–75 in Steven Dick (ed.) *Many Worlds* (Philadelphia and London: Templeton Foundation Press), 157.

66. P. J. Hess, "'God's Two Books': Revelation, Theology, and Natural Science in the Christian West," in *Interdisciplinary perspectives on cosmology and biological evolution*, H. D. Regan, M. Worthing (eds.), (Adelaide: Australian Theological Forum, 2002), 19–49.
67. C. Darwin, *The Origin of Species* (London: John Murray, 1859), chapter 14, 488, 490.
68. Throughout his adult life, Darwin journeyed from being a nominal Christian, to Deist, to being almost (but not quite) an agnostic, to theist.
69. Desmond and Moore, *Darwin*, 45–60.
70. H. Litchfield (ed.), *Emma Darwin: A Century of Family Letters*, 1792–1896, 2 vols, (New York: D. Appleton and Co., 1915, Vol 1), 206–10, 227. See also: N. Barlow (ed.), *The Autobiography of Charles Darwin* (London: Collins, 1958), 55. B. Wedgwood and H. Wedgwood, *The Wedgwood Circle* (Westfield, NJ: Eastview, 1980), 200.
71. Barlow, *The Autobiography of Charles Darwin*, 64–65.
72. Desmond and Moore, *Darwin*, 78,85.
73. Barlow, *The Autobiography of Charles Darwin*, 86.
74. Barlow, *The Autobiography of Charles Darwin*, 57.
75. Barlow, *The Autobiography of Charles Darwin*, 57,85.
76. Barlow, *The Autobiography of Charles Darwin*, 57.
77. Desmond and Moore, *Darwin*, 5–30.
78. Darwin did not have a unit of heredity that would explain how organisms inherited traits from earlier generations. That mechanism (genetics) would come later in 1900 when several plant breeders independently discovered the pioneering work of the Austrian monk Gregor Mendel in the 1860's.
79. Barlow, *The Autobiography of Charles Darwin*, 87.
80. The line, "nature red in tooth and claw"is part of a very long poem by Alfred Tennyson entitled "*In Memoriam: A. H. H.*" (parts 55–56) written in 1850, before Darwin published his ideas on evolution.
81. Darwin wrote to his friend Asa Gray in 1860 saying, "I had no intention to write atheistically. But I own that I cannot see as plainly as others, and as I should wish to do, evidence of design and beneficence on all sides of us. There seems to me too much misery in the world. I cannot persuade myself that a beneficent and omnipotent God would have designedly created the Ichneumonidae with the express intention of their feeding within the living bodies of caterpillars, or that a cat should play with mice." See: F. Darwin, *The Life and Letters of Charles Darwin*, .II, 2,:105. This can be viewed on: www.pages.britishlibrary,net/charles.darwin/texts/letters/letters2_02html.
82. C. Darwin, Letter to J. Hooker, 1870, in F. Darwin and A. C. Seward (eds.) *More Letters of Charles Darwin*, 2 vols, (New York: Appleton, 1903), Vol.1, 5:321. This can be viewed on: www.pages.britishlibrary,net/charles.darwin/texts/letters/letters1_fm.html.
83. Desmond and Moore, *Darwin*, 384. This episode has been treated in more detail by Randal Keynes in his book *Annie's Box* (London: Fourth Estate, 2001).
84. Barlow, *The Autobiography of Charles Darwin*, 87.
85. Desmond and Moore, *Darwin*, 80–82, 89–90. It is also worth noting that the heritage of Anglican clerical naturalists was to have a moderating affect on Darwin's passion for shooting. A Copy of Rev. Gilbert White's book *A Natural History of Selborne* began to teach Darwin "to treat birds less like moving targets" (Desmond and Moore, *Darwin*, 29).

86. Desmond and Moore, *Darwin*, 578,657.
87. Desmond and Moore, *Darwin*, 477,502.
88. Kingsley wrote a letter to Darwin in 1859 thanking him for sending him a copy of *The Origin of Species*. In his letter, Kingsley wrote that he found it "just as noble a conception of Deity to believe that He created primal forms capable of self development. . . " See: F. Darwin, *The Life and Letters of Charles Darwin*. 2 vols.,(New York: Appleton, 1898, Vol 2), 82.
89. Desmond and Moore, *Darwin*, 492-99.
90. Notwithstanding his friendship, Wilberforce's theological objection was probably strong enough for him not to approve of Palmerston's request that Darwin be given a knighthood as this honor would have implied approval of his thinking. (Desmond and Moore, *Darwin*, 488.)
91. Desmond and Moore, *Darwin*, 601. See also: A. E. McGrath, Science & Religion, 24-25.
92. F. Temple, *The Present Relations of Science to Religion*: A Sermon Preached on July 1, 1860 before the University of Oxford. See: J. Brooke and G. Cantor, *Reconstructing Nature*, 36.
93. J. Wentzel van Huyssteen, *Duet or Duel? Theology and Science in a Postmodern World*, (London: SCM, 1998), 86.
94. P. C. W. Davies, *The Mind of God: Science and the Search for Ultimate Meaning* (New York: Simon & Schuster Ltd., 1992), 20-21. Notwithstanding his previous comment, the reality of human existence persuades Paul Davies (a mathematical physicist with no conventional faith) to believe that humankind's existence is not a cosmic accident but that "we are truly meant to be here" (Davies, *The Mind of God*, 232.)
95. C. Darwin, *The Descent of Man* (London: John Murray, 1871), chapter 21, 395-96.
96. Barlow, *The Autobiography of Charles Darwin*, 91.
97. From a letter by Darwin to his wife and children, written in 1876. See: Barlow, *The Autobiography of Charles Darwin*, 164-65.
98. Barlow, *The Autobiography of Charles Darwin*, 92.
99. Darwin (ed.), *The Life and Letters of Charles Darwin*, 1.282.
100. Darwin (ed.), *The Life and Letters of Charles Darwin*, 1.304.
101. C. Darwin, *The Origin of Species* (London: Penguin Books, 1985), 458.
102. Darwin, *The Origin of Species*, 459. In later editions, the wording has been altered to read, "originally breathed by the Creator into . . . " but it is not sure whether this revision came from Darwin or not.
103. van Huyssteen, *Duet or Duel?* 95-98.
104. van Huyssteen, *Duet or Duel?* 99.
105. van Huyssteen, *Duet or Duel?* 103.
106. van Huyssteen, *Duet or Duel?* 100.
107. J. Durant (ed.), *Darwinism and Divinity*, (Oxford: Blackwell, 1985), 9.
108. Worthing, "Science and Theology—An Historical Overview," 9.
109. J. W. Draper, *History of the Conflict between Religion and Science* (London: Henry S. King, 1875), 367.
110. I. Barbour, *Issues in Science and Religion* (London: SCM Press, 1966)
111. Worthing, "Science and Theology—An Historical Overview," 10.
112. Some of these centers include: The Carl Howie Center for Science, Art and Theology (Union Theological Seminary and Presbyterian School of Christian Education, Richmond, Virginia); The Center for Theology and the Natural Sciences (Berkeley,

California); The Center for Research in Science (Azusa Pacific University, Los Angeles); The Center for the Renewal of Science and Culture (Seattle); The Center for Faith and Science Exchange (Boston Theological Institute); The Chicago Center for Religion and Science; The Institute for Theological Encounter with Science and Technology (St. Louis); The Pascal Center for Advanced Studies in Faith and Science (Redeemer College, Ontario, Canada); The Ian Ramsey Center (Oxford); Wycliffe Hall (Oxford); The Faraday Institute, St Edmunds College, Cambridge.

113. B. Edgar, "Order and Catastrophe: Science and Religion in Australia, 1828" pages 21–28 in *Pacific Journal of Theology and Science*, 1, (2000): 21.

CHAPTER 2

Science Allows Faith

1. Richard Dawkins, *The God Delusion*. (Boston, MA: Houghton Mifflin, 2006), p.31. Dawkins displays both a misunderstanding of the nature of Scripture and an ignorance of how Scripture should be used with integrity. The Scriptures show a progressive revelation of God's nature and purposes which reach their fullness in the teachings of Jesus Christ. As such, no verse of the Old Testament should be understood outside its context or outside the context of the consistent principles taught by all of Scripture. Even in the Old Testament, the teaching that God is a God of love, justice and integrity features very strongly (2 Chron 6:14; Jer 31:3; Hos 2:14). So much so, that it was a revolutionary concept at the time it was written.
2. Dawkins, *The God Delusion*, pp.112–13.
3. Fred Hoyle, "Hoyle On Evolution," *Nature* 294 (November 12, 1981):105.
4. N. Hawkes, *An Apology for the Scientific Credibility of Faith*, 48–49. This survey was conducted amongst 311 tertiary trained people.
5. J. Polkinghorne, *Belief in God in an Age of Science*, (Yale University Press, 1998), 77.
6. J. C. Puddefoot, *Logic and Affirmation: Perspectives in Mathematics and Theology*, (Edinburgh: Scottish Academic Press, 1987), 17.
7. A. R. Peacocke, *Intimations of Reality* (University of Nôtre Dame Press, 1984), 51.
8. S. J. Gould, *Dinosaur in a Haystack: Reflections in Natural History* (London: Johnathon Cape, 1996). The text is taken from his "Introduction". In more recent writings, Gould is more moderate in his views, see: S. J. Gould, *Rocks of Ages: Science and Religion in the Fullness of Life*, (New York: The Ballantyne Publishing Group, 1999), 49–67. In this book, Gould coins the acronym "NOMA" for "non-overlapping magisteria". This idea suggests that science and religion each be allowed to contribute in those domains for which that particular mode of thinking is most appropriate, and restricted from interfering in domains for which it is not.
9. P. C. W. Davies, *The Mind of God: Science and the Search for Ultimate Meaning* (New York: Simon & Schuster Ltd., 1992), 16,232.
10. D. MacKay, *Human Science and Human Dignity*: London Lectures in *Contemporary Christianity* (London: Hodder and Stoughton, 1979), 35.
11. S. Weinberg, *The First Three Minutes: A Modern View of the Origin of the Universe* (New York: Basic Books, 1977), 154.
12. F. Dyson, *Infinite in all Directions* (New York: Harper & Row, 1988), 117–18.

13. F. Dyson, *Disturbing the Universe* (New York: Harper & Row, 1979), 249–
14. R. H. Brown, *The Wisdom of Science: Its Relevance to Culture and Religion*, (Cambridge: Cambridge University Press, 1986), 161.
15. P. Medawar, *The Limits of Science* (Oxford: Oxford University Press, 1984), p.66.
16. J. D. Barrow *Impossibility: The Limits of Science and the Science of Limits*, (Oxford: Oxford University Press, 1998), 47–57.
17. W. Pannenberg, "Theological Questions to Scientists" pages 3–16 in A. R. Peacocke, (ed.) *The Sciences and Theology in the Twentieth Century*, (London: Oriel Press, 1981), 4.
18. Pannenberg, "Theological Questions to Scientists," 4.
19. Pannenberg, "Theological Questions to Scientists," 4.
20. T. F. Torrance, "Divine and Contingent Order," 87.
21. T. F. Torrance, "God and the Contingent World." *Zygon*, 14, (December 1979): 329–48.
22. A. Einstein, H. A. Lorentz, H. Minkowski, and H. Weyl, trans. W. Perrett and G. B. Jeffrey, *The Principle of Relativity* (London: Methuen and Company, Ltd., 1923) 175–88.
23. A number of names have been given to this new force including vacuum energy, anti-gravity and dark energy.
24. Einstein had divided both sides of an equation by a quantity which Friedman found could become zero under certain circumstances. Since division by zero is not permitted in algebraic computations, the possibility of a non static universe could not be ruled out.
25. E. Hubble, *The Realm of the Nebulae* (New Haven, Connecticut: Yale University Press, 1936), chapter V.
26. The term "Big Bang" was a pejorative title given by Fred Hoyle in 1950 who would not believe in the concept.
27. J. Trefil, *The Dark side of the Universe* (New York: Scribner's, 1988), 51.
28. Ferris, *The Whole Shebang*, 33–34
29. Ferris, *The Whole Shebang*, 166. Astronomer George Smoot led the research team that discovered the ripples in microwave background in 1992.
30. There have been a recent challenges to the theory of the Big Bang which stem from there being evidence for the existence of a period of cosmic inflation just prior to the big bang. This will be examined later.
31. Hoyle, *The Intelligent Universe*, 237.
32. Reported by J. D. Barrow and F. R. Tipler, *The Anthropic Cosmological Principle*, (New York: Oxford University Press, 1986), 107–8).
33. Cited in McMullin, "How Should Cosmology Relate to Theology?" 36, from Loren Graham, *Science and Philosophy in the Soviet Union*, (New York: Knopf, 1972), 173.
34. Cited in McMullin, "How Should Cosmology Relate to Theology?" 36, from Loren Graham, *Science and Philosophy in the Soviet Union*, 156.
35. J. Monod, *Chance and Necessity* trans, A. Wainhouse (Collins, London, 1972), 167.
36. R. J. Russell, "Intelligent Life in the Universe: Philosophical and Theological Issues" (working draft), Center for Theology and the Natural Sciences, Berkeley, U.S.A. www.ictp.trieste.it/~chelaf/lecture.html Robert Russell is Director of the Center for Theology and Natural Sciences in Berkeley.
37. R. Dawkins, *River Out of Eden*, (London: Phoenix, 1995), 133.

38. Polkinghorne, *Belief in God in an Age of Science*, 12.
39. Polkinghorne, Belief in God in an Age of Science, 14.
40. Some of Dawkins' books include *The Selfish Gene* (1976), *The Blind Watchmaker* (1986), *River out of Eden* (1995) and *Climbing Mount Improbable* (1996).
41. Dawkins, *The Selfish Gene*.
42. R. Dawkins, *Climbing Mount Improbable*, (New York: W.W. Norton & Co., 1996), 236.
43. F. Miele, "Darwin's Dangerous Disciple: An Interview with Richard Dawkins". Pages 80–85 in *Skeptic*, Vol 3, (1995): 84.
44. Dawkins, *River Out of Eden*, 155.
45. Dawkins, *River Out of Eden,* 183. See also: Dawkins, *Selfish Gene*, 59.
46. Miele, "Darwin's Dangerous Disciple," 85.
47. Ward, *God, Chance and Necessity*, 147.
48. Michael Behe is Professor of biochemistry at Lehigh University, Pennsylvania.
49. M. J. Behe, *Darwin's Black Box: The Biochemical Challenge to Evolution* (New York: Free Press, 1996), 31–36.
50. e.g., K. R. Miller, *Finding Darwin's God: A Scientist's Search for Common Ground Between God and Evolution* (New York: Perennial, an imprint of HarperCollins, 1999) 130–64. See also: R. T. Pennock, *Tower of Babel: The Evidence Against New Creationism*, (Cambridge, MA: The MIT Press, 2000).
51. It is known that some beetles use quinones to make themselves taste bad to prospective predators and that others use hydrogen peroxide for defensive purposes. The catalytic enzyme responsible for causing the chemicals to react is, in fact, quite common and is found in most living cells.
52. S. J. Gould, Ever Since Darwin (New York: Norton, 1979), 104).
53. Dawkins, *River out of Eden*, 98–103.
54. A. Peacocke, "The Challenge and Stimulus of the Epic of Evolution to Theology" pages 89–117 in S. Dick (ed.) *Many Worlds* (Philadelphia and London: Templeton Foundation Press, 2000), 92–96. One such scientist is Jonathan Wells who is a post-doctoral researcher at the University of California, Berkeley. Wells has a PhD. in molecular and cell biology from the University of California and a PhD. in religious studies from Yale. See: J. A. Wells, *Icons of Evolution: Science or Myth?* (Washington, DC: Regenery Publishing, 2000).
55. St. Augustine, *Confessions*, Book I.1.1. (See: www.ccel.org/paper.cgi?file=a/augustine/confessions).
56. See: T. LaHaye and D. A. Noebel, *Mind Siege: The Battle for the Truth in the New Millennium*, (Nashville, TN: Word Publishing, 2000), and: C. Matrisciana and R. Oakland, *The Evolution Conspiracy*, (Eugene, Oregon: Harvest House, 1991).
57. For example: J. Rennie, "15 Answers to Creationist Nonsense," pages 62–69 in *Scientific American*, 287 (July 2002). It should be appreciated that there are different levels of literalism. Michael Behe, author of *Darwin's Black Box* is not one who believes the earth was created in 4004 BC as suggested by some who hold to a strict literalist view of the Bible. Behe believes the earth is much older but nonetheless maintains that the existence of inexplicable complexity in life points to the possibility of intelligent design.
58. Ward, God, *Chance and Necessity*, 63, 65.
59. This discipline of scientific investigation has been called "methodological naturalism".

60. Much of this section was informed by a talk given by Dr David Wilkinson at Tabor College, Adelaide, South Australia, on 11th January, 2010. Dr David Wilkinson is Principal of St. John's College, Durham University.
61. This claim was popularized in the film *Footprints in Stone*, a film produced in 1973 by Stanley Taylor for Films for Christ Association, Inc. Mesa, AZ. The film has since been withdrawn. For more information, see: http://paleo.cc/paluxy/sor-ipub.htm.
62. J. Polkinghorne, *Science and Theology: An Introduction* (London: SPCK 1998), 71.
63. I. G. Barbour, *Religion in an Age of Science* (London: SCM, 1990), .4–30. Barbour develops these ideas further in his later book: I. G. Barbour, *When Science Meets Religion: Enemies, Strangers or Partners*, (San Francisco, CA: Harper, 2000).
64. S. J. Gould, *Rocks of Ages*.
65. Teilhard believes that God has implanted into primal particles of the universe an urge towards unity, greater complexity and consciousness. Subatomic particles therefore have a rudimentary consciousness. Particles and organisms have evolved until fully functioning human consciousness (noogenesis) occurred. Life will continue to develop until planetary consciousness occurs and everything is brought into union with God. This "Omega Point" is where the church becomes the body of Christ in a literal sense. See: P. Teilhard de Chardin, *Towards the Future* trans. R. Hague, (London: Collins, 1975).
66. James Lovelock promoted the idea of a global ecosystem. He argued that the global ecosystem should be regarded as an entity, even an organism, which he has named "Gaia". The earth's ecosystems interlock to create a global network of negative feedback systems which regulate the earth's being. Lovelock describes Gaia as: "A complex entity involving the Earth's biosphere, atmosphere, oceans, and soil; the totality constituting a feedback or cybernetic system which seeks an optimal physical and chemical environment for life on this planet." See: J. E. Lovelock, Gaia: *A new look at life on Earth*, (Oxford: Oxford University Press, 1979), 11.
67. See: C. Hartshorne, *Man's Vision of God*, (Chicago: Willet Clark, 1941).
68. See: J. B. Cobb, *Is it too late? A Theology of Ecology* (Beverly Hills, CA: Bruce, 1962).
69. C. Birch and J. B. Cobb, *The Liberation of Life: From the Cell to the Community*, (Cambridge: Cambridge University Press, 1981). Panentheism is a belief that God penetrates all created matter.
70. A. Peacocke, *God and Science: A Quest for Christian Credibility* (London: SCM, 1996), 22. Arthur Peacocke was the winner of the 2001 Templeton Prize for Progress in Religion.
71. J. Polkinghorne, *Scientists as Theologians* (London: SPCK, 1996), 6–7.
72. H. Rolston, "Science, Religion and the Future" in *Religion and Science: History, Method and Dialogue* ed. W. M. Richardson and W. J.Wildman, (London and New York: Routledge, 1996), 61f. John Polkinghorne suggests that biologists see a much more perplexing, disorderly and painful view of reality than that presented by the beautiful order of fundamental physics and that this may explain the difficulty biologists have in believing in divine order and purpose. See: Polkinghorne, *Belief in God in an Age of Science*, 65.
73. E. Peters, "Theology and Science: Where are We?" pages 325–31 in *Zygon* 31 (1996): 323–43.
74. F. Hoyle, *The Nature of the Universe* (Oxford: Blackwell, 1950), 110.
75. T. Ferris, *The Whole Shebang*, 21.
76. W. Heisenberg, *Physics and Beyond* (New York: Harper and Row, 1971), 83.

77. Polkinghorne, *Quarks, Chaos, and Christianity*, 12.
78. F. Watts (ed.), *Science Meets Faith: Theology and Science in Conversation* (London: SPCK, 1998), 13.
79. John Paul II (Pope) message to George V. Coyne, *Physics, Philosophy and Theology: A Common Quest for Understanding*, eds. R. J. Russell, W. R. Stoeger, SJ, and George V. Coyne, S.J (Vatican City State: Vatican Observatory, 1988), M13.
80. A. Einstein, "Science and Religion," *Ideas and Opinions* ed. Carl Seelig, (New York, Random House, 1995), 36–39. Einstein delivered this quote at a Symposium on Science, Philosophy and Religion in 1941. It was also published in *Nature* 146 (1941): 605. The geneticist R. J. Berry extends Einstein's remark from science to reason in general. He says, "Science and faith have different methodologies, but they are complementary, not contradictory; a faith without reason is as stultifying as a reason without faith." See: R. J. Berry, "Genes, Genesis, and Greens," pages 185–95 in R. J. Berry (ed.) *Real Science, Real Faith* (Crowborough: Monarch, 1991), 195.
81. J. Polkinghorne, *Reason and Reality: The Relationship between Science and Theology*, (London: SPCK, 1991), 75.
82. J. Polkinghorne, *Scientists as Theologians*, 6.
83. Polkinghorne, *Quarks, Chaos, and Christianity*, 13.
84. D. C. Burke, "Evolution and Creation" pages 42–58 in Fraser Watts (ed.), *Science Meets Faith: Theology and Science in Conversation* (London: SPCK, 1998), 56.
85. Polkinghorne, *Belief in God in an Age of Science*, 18.
86. Polkinghorne, *Belief in God in an Age of Science*, 19.
87. Polkinghorne, *Belief in God in an Age of Science*, 24.
88. Polkinghorne, *Quarks, Chaos, and Christianity*, 14.
89. G. H. Wheatley, "Constructivist Perspectives on Science and Mathematics Learning," pages 9–21 in *Science Education* 75 (Jan, 1991): 10.
90. E. von Glasersfeld, "Cognition, Construction of Knowledge, and Teaching," pages 121–40 in *Synthese* 80 (1989), 135.
91. Polkinghorne, *Belief in God in an Age of Science*, 104.
92. Wentzel van Huyssteen, *Theology and the Justification of Faith* (Grand Rapids, MI: Eerdmans, 1989), 162–63.
93. Polkinghorne, *Quarks, Chaos, and Christianity*, 67–68.
94. Polkinghorne, *Belief in God in an Age of Science*, 52–53.
95. Polkinghorne, *Belief in God in an Age of Science*, 53.
96. N. C. Murphy, "Relocating Theology and Science in a Postmodern Age," *CTNS Bulletin* (Berkeley, CA) 7 (Autumn 1987): 1–10.
97. S. W. Hawking, *A Brief History of Time* (London and New York: Bantam, 1988), 174.
98. Ferris, *The Whole Shebang*, 13.
99. Barbour, *Religion in an Age of Science*, 20.
100. Polkinghorne, *Belief in God in an Age of Science*, 15.
101. M. Polanyi, *Personal Knowledge: Towards a Post-Critical Philosophy* (London: Routledge & Kegan Paul, 1958), 214.
102. Polanyi, Personal Knowledge, 193–95; 252–55; 306–18. Lesslie Newbigin has expressed a similar point of view from a theological perspective in his book: L. Newbigin, *Foolishness to the Greeks*, (London: SPCK, 1986), chapter 4.
103. S. Toulmin, *The Return to Cosmology: Postmodern Science and the Theology of Nature*, (Berkeley, CA: University of California Press, 1985), 210, 237f.,

104. van Huyssteen, *Duet or Duel?* 16. Not only does the view of science vary from locality to locality but postmodern philosophy also recognizes that science itself is an historically dynamic process, (van Huyssteen, *Duet or Duel?* 16).
105. P. R. Gross and N. Levitt, *The Academic Left and its Quarrels with Science* (Baltimore: Johns Hopkins University Press, 1998), 40.
106. A. Sokal, "Transgressing the Boundaries: Toward a Transformative Hermeneutics of Quantum Gravity" *Social Text*, Spring-Summer, nos. 46–47, 1996.
107. A. Sokal. "A physicist experiments with cultural studies" *Lingua Franca*, May-June, 1996, pages 62–64.
108. This is indicated by the book: A. Sokal and J. Bricmont, *Intellectual Impostures: Postmodern Philosophers' abuse of science* (London: Profile Books, 1998). See also: P. R. Gross, N. Levitt and M. W. Lewis (eds.) *The Flight from Science and Reason* (Baltimore: Johns Hopkins University Press, 1997); and N. Koertge (ed.) *A House Built on Sand: Exposing Postmodernist Myths About Science* (New York and Oxford: Oxford University Press, 1998).
109. van Huyssteen, *Duet or Duel?* xii.
110. van Huyssteen, *Duet or Duel?* xii.
111. van Huyssteen, *Duet or Duel?* xiv–xv.
112. van Huyssteen, *Duet or Duel?* xvi.
113. MacKay, *Human Science and Human Dignity*, 113.
114. MacKay, *Human Science and Human Dignity*, 48.
115. In 1927, Werner Heisenberg showed that the more you sought to measure an electron's position, the less you could know about its momentum, i.e., what it was doing.
116. There is now an International Association for New Science, see: http://www.ians.org/. The origin of the term "new physics" is not easy to pinpoint. However, the development of its signature features are listed in two of the books by Sir James Jeans (the English mathematician, physicist and astronomer), see: J. H. Jeans, *Physics and Philosophy* (Cambridge: Cambridge University Press, 1948), and J. H. Jeans, *The Growth of Physical Science* (Cambridge: Cambridge University Press, 1947).
117. Dr. Francis Collins, in an interview with CNN on April 03, 2007. See also his book, *The Language of God: A Scientist Presents Evidence for Belief.* (New York, Simon & Schuster, 2007).

CHAPTER 3

Cosmic Order as Evidence for God

1. Paul Dirac "The Evolution of the Physicist's Picture of Nature." pages 45–53 in *Scientific American* 208 (1963): 47.
2. N. Hawkes, *An Apology for the Scientific Credibility of Faith*, (DMin Thesis), 84–86. This survey was conducted amongst 311 tertiary trained people who were non-church goers.
3. This was later published as: B. Carter, "Large Number Coincidences and the Anthropic Principle in Cosmology" *Confrontation of Cosmological Theories with Observational Data* ed. M. S. Longair (Holland, Dordrecht: Reidel, 1974).

4. Red dwarfs are smaller and cooler than our sun and are therefore less productive in forming the elements necessary to form life. Blue giants are bigger and hotter than our sun. Because they burn very quickly at such hot temperatures, they too are unable to produce the elements necessary for life.
5. Carter, "Large Number Coincidences," 291.
6. A good resource for this topic is: Barrow and Tipler, *The Anthropic Cosmological Principle*.
7. J. Polkinghorne, *Science and Theology: An Introduction*, (London: SPCK,1998), 74. The physicist John A. Wheeler is the most prominent person to write about the "participatory anthropic principle". See: J. A. Wheeler, "The Universe as Home for Man," pages 261–96 in O. Gingerich (ed.) *The Nature of Scientific Discovery*, (Washington: Smithsonian Institute Press, 1975). See also: J. A. Wheeler, *At Home in the Universe*, (New York: Springer-Verlag, 1992), 23–46.
8. The "participatory" version of the "strong" anthropic principle is only slightly different and says that the universe is observer dependent. Nothing exists until they are observed, see: Ferris, *The Whole Shebang*, 299.
9. Euclidian geometry requires the sum of a triangle's three angles to add up to 180 degrees.
10. Ferris, *The Whole Shebang*, 299.
11. Polkinghorne, *Science and Theology*, 74.
12. Polkinghorne, *Quarks, Chaos, and Christianity*, 27.
13. Hawking, *A Brief History of Time*, 291.
14. More information on the necessity for very precise numerical values of the factors and forces which have allowed life to develop can be seen in the book by Cambridge astronomer Martin Rees: M. Rees, *Just Six Numbers: The Deep Forces that Shape the Universe* (New York: Basic Books [Perseus Group], 2000).
15. Polkinghorne, *Quarks, Chaos, and Christianity*, 29.
16. Polkinghorne, *Quarks, Chaos, and Christianity*, 28–30.
17. Ferris, *The Whole Shebang*, 200. This state of affairs is what is known as a "frozen accident," it is not a law of nature, but an accident (apparently), the consequences of which have been frozen into nature ever since.
18. "God Only Knows" by *Oxford Television Company*, made for Channel 4, U.K., aired on ABC TV in April, 1999.
19. S. W. Hawking, *A Brief History of Time: From the Big Bang to Black Holes* (New York: Bantam, 1988), 122. Over ten million copies of this book have been sold, making it the most widely read book on cosmology. Hawkins' ambivalence toward Christianity may stem in part from the influence of his mother Isabel who was a member of the Communist Party in England, and the influence of Jane Wilde, a Christian, whom he married in 1965.
20. Stephen Hawking, quoted in: J. Boslough, *Stephen Hawking's Universe* (New York: Simon and Schuster, 1983), 30.
21. S. Hawking and L. Mlodinow, *The Grand Design* (New York, Bantam, 2010), p180.
22. J. Lennox in the *Daily Mail*, 3rd Sept 2010, see: www.dailymail.co.uk/debate/article-1308599
23. Davies, *The Mind of God*, 195.
24. Davies, *The Mind of God*, 21,148.
25. Polkinghorne, *Science and Theology*, 72.

26. Polkinghorne, *Science and Theology*, 73.
27. Polkinghorne, *Reason and Reality*, 37.
28. Polkinghorne, *Science and Theology*, 73.
29. J. Leslie, *Universes* (London; New York: Routledge, 1989), 9–13,198.
30. B. J. Carr and M. J. Rees, "The Anthropic Principle and the Structure of the Physical World," *Nature* 278, (1979): 605–12.
31. The periodic table lists all the atoms that exist in the universe. Elements are composed of just one type of atom.
32. A famous paper (called "B²FH" after the initials of its authors) was published in 1957: M. E. Burbridge, G. R. Burbridge, W. A. Fowler, and F. Hoyle "Synthesis of the Elements in Stars," pages 547–650 in Rev. Mod. Phys. 29, (1957).
33. F. Hoyle, "The Universe: Past and Present Reflections," pages 1–35 in *Annual Review of Astronomy and Astrophysics*, 20, (1982): 16. The lower energy level of the resonance in O_{16} means that carbon is only slowly transformed into oxygen: both are essential for life, and a higher energy level resonance would mean that most carbon would be rapidly converted into oxygen, leaving virtually no carbon behind.
34. The anthropic principle is based on the idea that any living organism will have the same chemical make-up as living organisms on Earth. In other words, it assumes that all life is "life as we know it". To date, at least, "life as we do not know it" is confined to the pages of science fiction.
35. Carr and Rees, "The Anthropic Principle and the Structure of the Physical World," 612.
36. See: R. Puccetti, *Persons: A Study of Possible Moral Agents in the Universe* (London: Macmillan, 1968).
37. Hawking, *A Brief History of Time*, 126.
38. Polkinghorne, *Quarks, Chaos, and Christianity*, 30.
39. Rees, *Before the Beginning*, 242.
40. This issue of God's relationship to time is discussed further in chapter 5.
41. C. S. Lewis, *Miracles, A Preliminary Study* (London: Geoffrey Bes, 1947), p.63.
42. More than 3,000 papers on the topic have been published since 1981. See: Horgan J. "Pinning Down Inflation," *Scientific American* 276 (June 1997):
43. Key researchers who helped to further refine the model include Andrei Linde and Paul Steinhardt.
44. Grand unified theories unite strong nuclear force with the electroweak theory, itself a unification of the weak nuclear force and electromagnetism. "Grand unified theories" preceded "string" and "membrane" theories. (See: Ferris, *The Whole Shebang*, 217–19.)
45. A. Linde "The Self-Reproducing Inflationary Universe," *Scientific American* (Nov., 1994). For an updated version of this paper on the Web, see: http://www.sciam.com/specialissues/0398cosmos/0398linde.html Andrei Linde is a graduate from Moscow University and the Lebedev Physics Institute in Moscow. He is now professor of physics at Stanford University.
46. A phase transition is the change between two states e.g., ice to water.
47. Scalar fields can be explained by the analogy of electrostatic potential in an electrical circuit. The electrical field only appears if the potential is uneven as it is between the poles of a battery. If the entire universe had the same electrostatic potential, nobody would notice and it would exist only as a vacuum state. Similarly, a constant scalar field looks just like a vacuum. We do not see it even though we are surrounded by it. (Linde, "The Self-Reproducing Inflationary Universe.")

48. Linde "The Self-Reproducing Inflationary Universe".
49. L. Smolin "Our Relationship to the Universe," pages 79–86 in S. Dick (ed.) *Many Worlds* (Philadelphia and London: Templeton Foundation Press, 2000), 84.
50. Smolin "Our Relationship to the Universe," 80.
51. Smolin "Our Relationship to the Universe," 85.
52. For example, in recent years, measurements of the density of matter in the universe have consistently come up short of the amount necessary to produce a flat universe. See: Horgan J. "Pinning Down Inflation," *Scientific American* 276 (June 1997): 17–19.
53. Linde, "The Self-Reproducing Inflationary Universe."
54. Hawking, A Brief History of Time, 1.
55. J. C. Eccles, The Human Mystery (London: Routledge and Kegan Paul, 1984), 13.
56. Polkinghorne, *Belief in God in an Age of Science*, 8–9.
57. For more on speculations about other life forms such as plasma life, see: Gerald Feinberg and Robert Shapiro, *Life Beyond Earth: The Intelligent Earthling's Guide to Life in the Universe* (New York: William Morrow, [an imprint of HarperCollins], 1980).
58. Polkinghorne, *Science and Theology*, 75.
59. Polkinghorne, *Science and Theology*, 74–75.
60. The extra dimensions (beyond the ones we recognize of three spatial dimensions and time) are thought to be compactified, or curled up, into tiny pockets inside observable space.
61. According to Edward Witten, who coined the phrase, "M" stands for "magic," "mystery" or "membrane," depending on your taste.
62. The idea that there were 11 dimensions had been postulated some years earlier by those working on super-gravity, e.g., Michael Duff, Professor of Physics at the University of Michigan. Duff was able to see that M-theory was able to embrace his super-gravity ideas along with those working on string theory. See: M. J. Duff, (ed.) *The World in Eleven dimensions: Super-gravity, super-membranes and M-Theory* (Philadelphia, PA.: IOP Publishing, 1999). For a good overview of the work on string theory and M-theory, see: B. R. Greene, *The Elegant Universe: Super-strings, Hidden Dimensions, and the Quest for the Ultimate Theory* (NY: Norton, 1999). Brian Green is professor of both Physics and Mathematics at Columbia University.
63. Eleven dimensions is the maximum allowed by super-symmetry of the elementary particles.
64. This idea was developed by Neil Turok of Cambridge University, Burt Ovrut of the University of Pennsylvania, and Paul Steinhardt and Justin Khoury of Princeton University.
65. Any experimental test of M-theory would involve such incredibly huge energies that it is far beyond the realms of any practical experiment in the foreseeable future.
66. Russell, "How the Heavens Have Changed," 7.
67. J. Polkinghorne, *Science and Christian Belief*, (London: SPCK, 1994), 70.
68. D. Darling, "On Creating something from nothing," *New Scientist*, 151 (1996), 49.
69. McMullin, "How Should Cosmology Relate to Theology?" 34.
70. McMullin, "How Should Cosmology Relate to Theology?" 38.
71. V. Trimble ,"Cosmology: Man's Place in the Universe". pages 76–86 in *American Scientist*, 65 (1977), 78.

72. See P. C. W. Davies "Biological Determinism, Information Theory, and the Origin of Life" pages 15–28 in Steven Dick (ed.) *Many Worlds* (Philadelphia and London: Templeton Foundation Press, 2000), 15, and S. J. Dick, "Cosmotheology: Theological Implications of the New Universe," pages 191–210 in S. Dick (ed.) *Many Worlds* (Philadelphia and London: Templeton Foundation Press, 2000), 206.
73. D. W. Singer, *Giordano Bruno, his Life and Thought*, (New York: Schuman, 1950). Singer's work also contains an annotated translation of *On the Infinite Universe and Worlds*.
74. See: M. J. Crowe, "A History of the Extraterrestrial Life Debate," *Zygon* 32, (1997): 147–62.
75. Thomas Aquinas, Summa Theologiae, 3, q.3, a.7. See D. Edwards, "Extraterrestrial Life and Jesus Christ," Pacific Journal of Theology and Science 1 (2000): 12–20.
76. Bonaventure, *Commentary on the Sentences*, 1. 44. 1, q.4, cited in Edwards, "Extraterrestrial Life and Jesus Christ," 13.
77. P. Melanchthon, *Initia doctrina physica*, Corpus Reformatorum 13.1.221, cited in D. Edwards, "Extraterrestrial Life and Jesus Christ". Pages 12–20 in *Pacific Journal of Theology and Science*, 1, (2000): 14.
78. Edwards, "Extraterrestrial Life and Jesus Christ," 15–16.
79. K. Rahner, *Foundations of Christian Faith* (New York: Crossroad, 1978), 283–84.
80. Edwards, "Extraterrestrial Life and Jesus Christ," 16–17.
81. Edwards, "Extraterrestrial Life and Jesus Christ," 19. Whilst this is so, the fact that God chose to reveal himself as the man Jesus says something of our significance to God. In other words, it is not that humankind has sought to make God in his own image but that God chose to reveal himself as the man, Jesus.
82. K. Rahner, "Natural Science and Reasonable Faith," *Theological Investigations* XXI (New York: Seabury Press, 1988), 51.
83. T. Paine, *The Age of Reason* (1793) in E. Foner, (ed.) Thomas Paine: *Collected Writings* (New York: Library of America, 1995), 710.
84. The Jesuit Karl Rahner (1904–1984) believed that God gives himself in self communication to human experience and is present in the transcendental experience of all human beings. As such, salvation though Christ can be realized without necessarily having knowledge of the historical Christian revelation. These "anonymous Christians" can be adherents of other faiths or even atheists who fail to thematize their transcendental relatedness as relation to God but who have not rejected it, see: L. J. O'Donovan, *A World of Grace: An Introduction to the Themes and Foundations of Karl Rahner's Theology* (New York: Seabury Press, 1984).
85. Edwards, "Extraterrestrial Life and Jesus Christ," 13.
86. Edwards, "Extraterrestrial Life and Jesus Christ," 14. Further information about Timothy Dwight's ideas on extra-terrestrial life can be found in Michael J. Crowe, *The Extraterrestrial Life Debate, 1750–1900* (New York: Dover Publications, 1999), 175–178.
87. P. Davies "Biological Determinism, Information Theory, and the Origin of Life," pages 15–28 in *Many Worlds: The New Universe, Extraterrestrial Life, and the Theological Implications* ed. S. J. Dick, (Philadelphia and London: Templeton Foundation Press, 2000), 26–27.
88. Ferris, *The Whole Shebang*, 293.
89. E. Mayr, *Toward a New Philosophy of Biology* (Cambridge: Harvard University Press, 1988), 73.

90. These programs are currently looking for evidence for "intelligent" life in the swath of electromagnetic radiation that bathes our planet from outer space. They look for evidence of this radiation being modified by the deliberate intervention of intelligent agents (much as humankind has modified them, e.g., with radio waves).
91. A term sometimes used when discussing the movement of life forms between planets is "panspermia" (a word coined by the distinguished Swedish chemist Svante August Arrhenius [1859 – 1927]). An early proponent of this was Lord Kelvin who said, "we must regard it as probable in the highest degree that there are countless seed-bearing meteoric stones moving through space." See: William Thomson (Lord Kelvin) "The Structure of Matter and the Unity of Science," pages 98–128 in G. Basalla, W. Colman and R. H. Kargon (eds.) *Victorian Science: A Self-Portrait from the Presidential Addresses of the British Association for the advancement of Science* (New York: Doubleday, 1970), 127.
92. Dr. Imre Friedmann, a NRC senior research fellow at NASA's Ames Research Center, reported this at the National Academy of Sciences on 27th February, 2001.
93. Magnetite is a magnetic form of iron oxide.
94. David McKay, scientist at NASA's Johnson Space Center, reported this to the Space and Aeronautics Committee on Science, U.S. House of Representatives, on September 12, 1996.
95. A nanometer is a millionth of a millimeter.
96. Uwins reported this finding at the Microelectronics Conference held in Adelaide in December, 2001.
97. Enrico Fermi's "Where are they" argument is reviewed in W. Sullivan, *We Are Not Alone*, revised ed. (New York: Penguin Books, 1993), 241–42.
98. J. C. Tarter "SETI and the Religions of the Universe" pages 143–49 in S. Dick (ed.) *Many Worlds* (Philadelphia and London: Templeton Foundation Press, 2000), 145.
99. S. von Hoerner, "The Likelihood of Interstellar Colonization and the Absence of Evidence," B. Zuckerman, and M. H. Hart, *Extraterrestrials, Where Are They?* 2nd ed., (Cambridge University Press, 1995), 29–31.
100. A. Moore, "The Christian Doctrine of God," in C. Gore (ed.) *Lux Mundi*, 12th ed. (London: John Murray, 1891), 73.
101. Davies, *The Mind of God*, 16.
102. R. Jastrow, *God and the Astronomers* (New York: W.W. Norton, 1978), 116.

CHAPTER 4

Cosmic Disorder as Evidence Against God

1. S. Harris, *The End of Faith* (New York: W.W. Norton, 2004).
2. S. Harris, *Letter to a Christian Nation* (New York: A.A. Knopf, 2006).
3. N. Hawkes, *An Apology for the Scientific Credibility of Faith*, 124–25. The questionnaire was conducted amongst 311 tertiary trained people who were not church goers.
4. Polkinghorne, *Science and Theology*, 76–77.
5. F. Darwin, *The Life and Letters of Charles Darwin*, Vol.II, Chapter 2, 105.
6. A planetesimal is a body in space formed by gravitational attraction between clumps of dust grains.

7. The Cambrian explosion in the number of complex species was made possible one to two billion years ago when the carbon–dioxide/nitrogen atmosphere gave way to oxygen/nitrogen.
8. O. Gingerich, "Is There Design and Purpose in the Universe?" pages 121–32 in J. F. Haught (ed.) *Science and Religion: In Search of Comic Purpose* (Washington, DC: Georgetown University Press, 2000), 127–28.
9. Gingerich, "Is There Design and Purpose in the Universe?" 129.
10. See: P. F. Boller, *American Thought in Transition: The Impact of Evolutionary Naturalism, 1865–1900.* (Chicago: Rand McNally, 1969). The Greek philosopher Empedocles (493–435 BC) has been called the father of evolutionary naturalism. He postulated the idea that chance alone was responsible for the development of humankind and that all living organisms gradually evolved by a process of trial-and-error recombinations of animal parts. See: H. F. Osborn, *From the Greeks to Darwin*, (New York: Charles Scribner's Sons, 1929), 52.
11. U. Goodenough, *The Sacred Depths of Nature* (New York; Oxford: Oxford University Press, 1998), 9–13.
12. C. De Duve "Lessons of Life" pages 3–13 in S. Dick (ed.) *Many Worlds* (Philadelphia and London: Templeton Foundation Press, 2000), 10–11. (De Duve won the 1974 Nobel Laureate in Medicine).
13. S. Fox and K. Dose, *Molecular Evolution and the Origin of Life* (New York: Marcel Dekker, 1977).
14. De Duve "Lessons of Life," 5.
15. De Duve "Lessons of Life," 5.
16. De Duve "Lessons of Life," 6–8.
17. Davies, "Biological Determinism, Information Theory, and the Origin of Life," 15.
18. T. Torrance, *Divine and Contingent Order* (Oxford University Press, 1981),
19. See: M. Eigen, *Steps Towards Life*, trans. P. Woolley (Oxford: Oxford University Press, 1992).
20. Davies, "Biological Determinism, Information Theory, and the Origin of Life," 19.
21. B. O. Küppers, "The World of Biological Complexity; Origin and Evolution of Life," pages 31–43 in Steven Dick (ed.) *Many Worlds* (Philadelphia and London: Templeton Foundation Press, 2000), 40.
22. Reported in: Peacocke, "The Challenge and Stimulus of the Epic of Evolution to Theology," 94.
23. Davies "Biological Determinism, Information Theory, and the Origin of Life," 19–20.
24. Davies "Biological Determinism, Information Theory, and the Origin of Life," 26–27.
25. The discoveries of Einstein have dethroned time and space from Newton's absolute unvarying prescriptive role in favor of the concept of the continuous field of space-time which interacts with the constituent matter/energy of the universe. This requires scientists and theologians to take seriously the existence of a universe that is, to some extent, continuously inventing itself.
26. T. F. Torrance, "Divine and Contingent Order," 86.
27. Torrance, "Divine and Contingent Order," 84. Langdon Gilkey also says that even the activity of knowing "points beyond itself to a ground of ultimacy which its own forms of discourse cannot usefully thematize, and for which religious symbolization is alone adequate". See: L. Gilkey, *Religion and the Scientific Future* (San Fanscisco: Harper, 1970), 41.

28. Torrance, "Divine and Contingent Order," 85.
29. Davies, *The Mind of God*, 92.
30. Davies, *The Mind of God*, 15.
31. Torrance, "Divine and Contingent Order," 81.
32. Torrance, "Divine and Contingent Order," 83.
33. Torrance, "Divine and Contingent Order," 83.
34. T. F. Torrance, *Preaching Christ Today; The Gospel and Scientific Thinking* (Grand Rapids, Michigan: Eerdmans, 1994), 64.
35. The energy levels of the resonance are not something imposed on the nuclei but are the consequences of the interactions between the quarks and gluons making up the nuclei, as described by quantum chromodynamics, see: L. Lederman with D. Teresi, *The God Particle: If the Universe Is the Answer, What is the Question?*, (New York: Bantam Doubleday, 1993), 334–41.
36. Gingerich, "Is There Design and Purpose in the Universe?" 125–126.
37. Gingerich, "Is There Design and Purpose in the Universe?" 129.
38. Polkinghorne, *Science and Theology: An Introduction*, 78.
39. Polkinghorne, *Belief in God in an Age of Science*, 5.
40. Polkinghorne, *Scientists as Theologians*, 46.
41. Polkinghorne, *Belief in God in an Age of Science*, 72,75.
42. Polkinghorne, *Belief in God in an Age of Science*, 74.
43. Gingerich, "Is There Design and Purpose in the Universe?" 130. The real issue is how much freedom has God given us. If God has not given us a plan which destiny must slavishly follow in all its detail, how much freedom God has given us? This will be examined further in chapter 5.
44. For example: Charles Harshorne's doctrine of "panpsychism," see: C. Hartshorne, "Panpsychism," *A History of Philosophical Systems* ed. V. Ferm, (New York: Rider and Company, 1950), 442–53, and David Ray Griffin's "panexperientialism," see: D. R. Griffin, *Unsnarling the World-Knot: Consciousness, Freedom, and the Mind-Body Problem* (Berkeley, CA: University of California Press, 1998).
45. See: A. N. Whitehead, Process and Reality: An Essay in Cosmology, (Cambridge, Cambridge University Press, 1929).
46. Whitehead believes that inanimate objects such as rocks and cars are aggregates of actual entities. As such it is their constituent entities rather than the object itself that are able to feel or experience.
47. This is not to suggest that God will eventually inaugurate a better coming kingdom. Rather, Whitehead postulates the existence of an infinite sequence of differing "cosmic epochs," in a universe which has no end.
48. Stromatolites are layered sedimentary structures produced by microorganisms.
49. C. P. McKay, "Astrobiology: The Search for Life Beyond the Earth," pages 45–58 in S. Dick (ed.) *Many Worlds* (Philadelphia and London: Templeton Foundation Press, 2000), 49–51.
50. Polkinghorne, *Belief in God in an Age of Science*, 72.
51. Polkinghorne, *Belief in God in an Age of Science*, 60.
52. E. N. Lorenz, "Deterministic non-periodic flow," pages 130–41 in *Journal of the Atmospheric Sciences*. 20, (1963). This thinking has led Philosopher John Leslie to muse whether moving an individual animal in the Cambrian seas two feet to its left could have meant that the conquest of land would not have occurred. See: J. Leslie "Intelligent Life in Our Universe," pages 119–32 in Steven Dick (ed.) *Many Worlds*, (Philadelphia and London: Templeton Foundation Press, 2000), 119.

53. Jim Yorke, an applied mathematician from the University of Maryland was the first to use the name Chaos for what, it transpired, was not even a chaos situation. Nonetheless, the name caught on, see: T. Y. Li, and J. A. Yorke, "Period Three Implies Chaos." *American Mathematical Monthly* 82, (1975): 985-92.
54. Polkinghorne, *Belief in God in an Age of Science*, 61, 63.
55. Dick, "Cosmotheology: Theological Implications of the New Universe," 204.
56. A.N Whitehead, *Process and Reality* ed. D. R. Griffin and D. W. Sherburne, (New York: Free Press, 1978), 348.
57. Polkinghorne, *Belief in God in an Age of Science*, 69-71.
58. G. Jantzen, *God's World, God's Body* (Philadelphia: Westminster Press, 1984)
59. Barbour, *Religion in an Age of Science*, 227.
60. Barbour, *Religion in an Age of Science*, 232-42.
61. Barbour, *Religion in an Age of Science*, 29, 224, 232, 264.
62. Barbour, *Religion in an Age of Science*, 264.
63. A. R. Peacocke, *Theology for a Scientific Age: Being and Becoming—Natural, Divine and Human*, (London: SCM and Minneapolis: Fortress Press, 1993), 65-67.
64. E. O. Wilson, Sociobiology: *The New synthesis* (Cambridge: Harvard University Press, 1975), 4.
65. Polkinghorne, *Science and Christian Belief*, 22-23.
66. Polkinghorne, *Scientists as Theologians*, 33.
67. Polkinghorne, *Scientists as Theologians*, 33.
68. Polkinghorne, *Belief in God in an Age of Science*, 56.
69. Polkinghorne, *Quarks, Chaos, and Christianity*, 73-74.
70. Polkinghorne, *Quarks, Chaos, and Christianity*, 74-75.
71. K. Barth, *Church Dogmatics*, Vol 1, I The Doctrine of the Word of God, (T & T. Clark, Edinburgh, 1936), 340.
72. Barth, Church Dogmatics, Vol 1, I *The Doctrine of the Word of God*, 369. Barth's distancing of God's nature from any human input is rescued from promoting the Greek idea of God being immutable and *apatheia* (unable to feel) by his emphasis on God being with us in the pain and challenges of life as the Word incarnate, Christ Jesus.
73. Polkinghorne, *Science and Creation*, 1.
74. Polkinghorne, *Belief in God in an Age of Science*, 13.

CHAPTER 5

Theology Completes Science

1. Polkinghorne, *Scientists as Theologians*, 44.
2. Hawking, *A Brief History of Time*, 141.
3. Ferris, *The Whole Shebang*, 194-195.
4. Ferris, *The Whole Shebang*, 309.
5. Ferris, *The Whole Shebang*, 202. (emphasis in the original).
6. Ferris, *The Whole Shebang*, 311.
7. Ferris, *The Whole Shebang*, 312
8. Peacocke, "The Challenge and Stimulus of the Epic of Evolution to Theology," 107.
9. Peacocke, "The Challenge and Stimulus of the Epic of Evolution to Theology," 97-98.

10. Polkinghorne, *Belief in God in an Age of Science*, 21.
11. W. Shakespeare, *Macbeth*, Act 5, Scene 5
12. R. J. Russell, "How the Heaven's Have Changed," pages 3–10 in *CTNS Bulletin* (Berkeley, CA), Vol 19, No 3, (1999): 5.
13. A. Einstein, "Physics and Reality," *Ideas and Opinions* (New York: Random House, 1988), 292.
14. Darwin said (as seen in chapter 1) "Believing as I do that man in the distant future will be a far more perfect creature than he now is, it is an intolerable thought that he and all other sentient beings are doomed to complete annihilation after such long-continued slow progress." See: Barlow, *The Autobiography of Charles Darwin*, 92.
15. Polkinghorne, *Scientists as Theologians*, 6–7.
16. The implication for Christian ideas about eschatology of two scientific scenarios for the end of the universe, 1) continual expansion and "heat death," or 2) eventual collapse and the "big crunch," have been examined by Mark Worthing in " M. Worthing, *God, Creation, and Contemporary Physics*, (Minneapolis: Fortress Press, 1996), chapter 5.
17. This earthquake measured 8.6 on the Richter scale. Whilst 15,000 died in Lisbon (a city of 250,000) the earthquake was eventually responsible for over 50,000 deaths over the whole region affected not only by the earthquake but by the resultant fires and tsunamis that followed it. For more information, see: T. D. Kendrick, *The Lisbon Earthquake* (London: Methuen & Co. Ltd., 1956).
18. A. R. Peacocke, *Intimations of Reality*, 63.
19. A. R. Peacocke "The Cost of New Life," pages 21–42 in J. Polkinghorne (ed.) *The Work of Love: Creation as Kenosis* (Grand Rapids, MI: Eerdmans, 2001), 23–35.
20. Barbour, *Religion in an Age of Science*, 28–29.
21. I. G. Barbour, "God's Power: A Process View," pages 1–20 in J. Polkinghorne (ed.) *The Work of Love: Creation as Kenosis* (Grand Rapids, MI: Eerdmans, 2001), 2–5.
22. A similar idea is expressed by John Hick who talks about this world being the vale of soul making, see: J. Hick, *Evil and the Love of God* (San Francisco, CA: Harper and Row, 1966).
23. J. Polkinghorne, "Kenotic Creation and Divine Action," pages 90–106 in John Polkinghorne (ed.) *The Work of Love: Creation as Kenosis* (Grand Rapids, MI: Eerdmans, 2001), 91–99.
24. Polkinghorne, *Quarks, Chaos, and Christianity*, 45.
25. Polkinghorne, *Quarks, Chaos, and Christianity*, 42–49.
26. Clark Pinnock was professor emeritus of theology at McMaster Divinity College, Hamilton, Ontario. John Sanders is professor of philosophy and religion at Huntington College, Indianapolis. Greg Boyd is a pastor and a consultant theologian to the American Baptist General Convention.
27. G. A. Boyd, *God of the Possible: A Biblical Introduction to the Open View of God* (Grand Rapids, MI: Baker, 2000), 31.
28. C. H. Pinnock, *Most Moved Mover: A Theology of God's Openness* (Carlisle, U.K.: Paternoster Press, 2001), 141–43.
29. God being impassable means that nothing can hurt him or act upon him. He acts solely out of his grace and mercy. God being omniscient means that God knows all the past, present and future.
30. The relational language of sun, moon stars etc. in Psalm 148 is understood to be poetic license

31. Einstein completed his General Theory of Relativity in 1915 (after 10 years of work). His last insights to this theory included the discovery that space, time, matter and energy were interrelated.
32. Because God is like this, we can say that God is truly "good" because God chooses to be good. If it were impossible for God to be anything other than good, then God not lying would not be a true good that comes from moral choice.
33. A. J. Freddoso, "The Openness of God: A Reply to William Hasker," at: http://www.opentheism.org/freddoso.htm Impassible means that nothing can hurt God or act upon him. Immutable means "unchangeable".
34. C. H. Pinnock, "God's sovereignty in today's world," *Theology Today* (Princeton Theological Library: N.J.) Vol 53, Issue 1, Apr (1996): 15f.
35. P. S. Fiddes, *Participating in God: A Pastoral Doctrine of the Trinity* (London: Darton, Longman and Todd, 2000), 122.
36. P. Helm, "Divine Timeless Eternity," pages 28–60 in G. E. Ganssle (ed.), *Four Views: God and Time* (Downers Grove, Ill: InterVarsity Press, 2001), 58–59.
37. Polkinghorne, *Belief in God in an Age of Science*, 14–15.
38. P. Tillich, *Systematic Theology*, 3 vols. (Chicago: Univ. of Chicago Press, 1951–63), 2:29.
39. Tillich, *Systematic Theology*, 2:47.
40. C. J. Armbruster, *The Vision of Paul Tillich* (New York: Sheed and Ward, 1967), 171.
41. Tillich, *Systematic Theology*, 2:43.
42. Despite all of creation being in "bondage to decay," God's creation nonetheless still shows some of God's glory. Despite the intrusion of sin and its marring effects on nature, there remains in creation a witness to the "eternal power and divine nature" of God (Rom 1:19-20).
43. R. Warren, *The Purpose Driven Church* (Grand Rapids: Zondervan, 1995), 361.
44. God may use suffering to refine us (Ps 66:8-12; Jas 1:2-4), to bring about some higher purpose (Jn 9:1-3; Phil 1:12-13) or to bring him glory through our faithfulness in the midst of suffering (Job 1:8-12; 2:3-6, 13:15).
45. W. W. Willis, *Theism, Atheism, and the Doctrine of the Trinity*, (Atlanta, Georgia: Scholars Press, 1987), 3.
46. Protest theism was also given definition by the likes of Ludwig Feuerbach, Friedrich Nietzsche and Jean Paul Sartre.
47. Willis, *Theism, Atheism, and the Doctrine of the Trinity*, 3.
48. A. Camus, *The Plague*, trans. Stuart Gilbert (New York, 1948), 196–97. The nineteenth century Russian novelist Fyodor Dostoevsky also explores this issue in his book *The Brothers Karamazov* (first published in 1880) when the socialist brother, Ivan, expresses a sentiment similar to Dr. Rieux to his brother Aloysha, a monk. See: F. Dostoevsky *The Brothers Karamozov*, ed. M. Komroff, trans. C.Garnett, (New York: Random House, 1996,), V.4, 263–72.
49. C. S. Lewis *A Grief Observed* (London: Faber and Faber, 1966), 56.
50. J. Moltmann, *The Crucified God: The Cross as the Foundation and Criticism of Christian Theology*, trans. R. A. Wilson and J. Bowden (London: SCM Press, 1974), 253.
51. It must be made clear that Jesus loved and honored those who were sick and disabled, but that he treated the disease or disability that afflicted them as an enemy to be overcome.

52. Willis, *Theism, Atheism and the Doctrine of the Trinity*, 87.
53. Discipleship of Christ can be costly, even deadly, for Christians are called to witness to Christ and stand alongside those for whom God expresses particular partiality, i.e., the poor, the outcast, the handicapped and the voiceless.
54. M. Lamb, *Solidarity with Victims: Toward a Theology of Social Transformation* (New York: Crossroad Publishing Co., 1982), 9–10.
55. I would want to broaden the definition of those needing ministry so that it is wider than that commonly employed by liberation theologians. There is need to include everyone who is suffering, powerless, ignorant of the gospel or not evidencing the gospel in their lives.
56. G. D. Fee, *Paul, the Spirit, and the People of God* (Hendrickson, 1996), 21,183.
57. Fee, *Paul, the Spirit, and the People of God*, 4,145.
58. Polkinghorne, "Kenotic Creation and Divine Action," 93.
59. Polkinghorne, *Reason and Reality*, 99.
60. A. G. Padgett, "Eternity As Relative Timelessness," pages 92–110 in Gregory E. Ganssle (ed.), *Four Views: God and Time* (Downers Grove, Ill: InterVarsity Press, 2001), 105. Alan Padgett is a theologian at Luther Seminary, St. Paul, Minnesota.
61. Padgett, "Eternity As Relative Timelessness," 100.
62. It is perhaps significant that Polkinghorne notes that despite the fall, the success of science in reading the Book of Nature "encourages the thought that humanity is not wholly benighted in the exercise of its rational faculties" (Polkinghorne, *Reason and Reality*, 101). In saying this, Polkinghorne seems to equate humankind's moral fallen state with humankind's rational fallen state which is not necessarily the same thing.
63. Recent testimony for this has been given in two videos produced by George Otis Jr.: G. Otis, *Transformations*: A documentary (video) (Seattle, WA: The Sentinel Group, 1999) and *Transformations II*: The Glory Spreads (video) (Seattle, WA: The Sentinel Group, 2001).

CHAPTER 6

Conclusion

1. J. Stenhouse, "Response to Norma Emerton's paper, 'arguments for the existence of God from nature and science,'" pages 87–96 in *Science and Theology: Question at the Interface*, M. Rae; H. Regan and J. Stenhouse (eds.), (Edinburgh: T&T Clark, 1994), 88–89.
2. C. Hyers *The Meaning of Creation: Genesis, and Modern Science*, (Atlanta, Georgia: John Knox Press, 1984), 26. Conrad Hyers is professor of comparative mythology and the history of religions at Gustavux Adolphus College, St. Peter, Minnesota.
3. *Unlocking the Mystery of Life: The Scientific Case for Intelligent Design* is produced by Illustra Media, and is promoted by the Discovery Institute, (based in Seattle, Washington, USA) a leading think tank on Intelligent Design.
4. The petition was at: http://www.ShovelBums.org.
5. This federal court case, run between September 26th and November 4th, was sometimes referred to as the "Scopes II" or the "Dover Panda Trial" by the media.

6. For a more detailed look at Millar's argument, see: Kenneth R. Miller, "The Flagellum Unspun: The Collapse of 'Irreducible Complexity'" in *Debating Design: From Darwin to DNA*, eds. W. A. Dembski & M. Ruse, (New York: Cambridge University Press, 2004), 81–97.
7. Fred Hoyle, "The Universe: Past and Present Reflections" *Engineering and Science*, (November, 1981): 8–12.
8. Francis Darwin (ed.) *The Life and Letters of Charles Darwin*, 2 vols (London, 1887, Vol.1), 304.
9. Albert Einstein, quoted in *Nature* 146 (1941), 605.
10. Paul Davies, *The Mind of God*, 16.
11. Stephen Hawking, quoted in: J. Boslough, *Stephen Hawking's Universe*, 30.

Bibliography

Aquinas, T. *Summa Theologica.* First part, Question 2, Article 3. (see: www.newadvent.org/summa/100203.htm)
Armbruster, C. J. *The Vision of Paul Tillich.* New York: Sheed and Ward, 1967.
Augustine, *Confessions,* I.1 and II.14, trans. R. S. Pine-Coffin, London: Penguin, 1961.
Augustine, *City of God,* trans. H. Bettenson, (Harmondsworth: Penguin Books, 1972) Book XI.
Augustine, *De Genesi ad Litteram.* I.18.37; I.20.40; I.21; II. 9; V.5; V.23. in: J. H. Taylor (trans.), *The Literal Meaning of Genesis,* 2 vols., Ancient Christian Writers series, No. 41,42, (New York: Newman Press, 1982).
Bacon, F. *The Advancement of Learning* (1605). London: Dent, 1965.
Barbour, I. G. *Issues in Science and Religion.* London: SCM Press, 1966.
———. *Religion in an Age of Science.* London: SCM Press, 1990.
Barbour, I. G. *When Science Meets Religion: Enemies, Strangers or Partners.* San Francisco, CA: Harper, San Francisco, 2000.
———. "God's Power: A Process View," in John Polkinghorne (ed.) *The Work of Love: Creation as Kenosis.* Grand Rapids, MI.: Eerdmans, 2001, 1–20.
Barlow, N. (ed.), *The Autobiography of Charles Darwin.* London: Collins, 1958.
Barrow, J. D. and Tipler, F. R. *The Anthropic Cosmological Principle.* New York: Oxford University Press, 1986.
———. *Impossibility: The Limits of Science and the Science of Limits.* Oxford: Oxford University Press, 1998.
Barth, K. *Church Dogmatics,* Vol. 1, I, *The Doctrine of the Word of God.* Edinburgh: T & T. Clark, 1936.
Battles, F. L. "God was accommodating Himself to Human Capacity," *Interpretation,* 31 (1977): 19–38.
Behe, M. J. *Darwin's Black Box: The Biochemical Challenge to Evolution.* New York: Free Press, 1996.
Berry, R. J. "Genes, Genesis, and Greens," in R. J. Berry (ed.) *Real Science, Real Faith.* Crowborough: Monarch, 1991, 185–95.
Birch, C. and Cobb, J. B. *The Liberation of Life: From the Cell to the Community.* Cambridge: Cambridge University Press, 1981.
Blackwell, J. J. *Galileo, Bellarmine, and the Bible.* Notre Dame, In: University of Notre Dame Press, 1991.
Boller, P. R. *American Thought in Transition: The Impact of Evolutionary Naturalism, 1865–1900.* Chicago: Rand McNally, 1969.
Bornkamm, H. *Luther's World of Thought.* Trans. M. H. Bertram, Saint Louis, MO: Concordia Publishing House, 1958.
Boslough, J. *Stephen Hawking's Universe.* New York: Simon and Schuster, 1983.

Boyd, G. A. *God of the Possible: A Biblical Introduction to the Open View of God*. Grand Rapids, MI: Baker, 2000.

Boyle, R. *Some Motives and Incentives to the Love of God* (1648) reprinted in 1659 (also known by the running title *Seraphick Love*, now available as: R. Boyle, *Serphic Love*, Belle Fourche, SD: Kessinger Publishing, 1992).

———. *The Excellency of Theology Compared with Natural Theology* (tract, 1674), cited at: www.neon.mems.cmu.edu/laughlin/Jub.1.pdf

Brooke, J. and Cantor, G. *Reconstructing Nature: The Engagement of Science and Religion*. Edinburgh: T&T Clark, 1988.

Brown, R. H. *The Wisdom of Science: Its Relevance to Culture and Religion*. Cambridge: Cambridge University Press, 1986.

Browne, T. *Religio Medici* (1642) ed. J. Winney, Cambridge: Cambridge University Press, 1983, part I, section 16, 1819.

Brundell, B. "Bellarmine to Foscarini on Copernicanism: A Theologian's Response," in G. Freeland and A. Corones (eds.), *1543 and All That*. Great Britain: Kluwer Academic Publishers, 2000, 375–93.

Burbridge, M. E. Burbridge, G. R., Fowler, W. A., and Hoyle, F., "Synthesis of the Elements in Stars". *Rev. Mod. Phys.* 29, (1957): 547–650.

Burke, D. C. "Evolution and Creation". Ed. Fraser Watts, *Science Meets Faith: Theology and Science in Conversation*. London: SPCK, 1998, 42–58.

Burkhardt, F. and Smith, S. (eds.) *The Correspondence of Charles Darwin 1821–1882*. Cambridge: Cambridge University Press, 1985.

Calvin, J. *Commentaries: Genesis*, Grand Rapids, Michigan; Baker Book House. See also: J. Calvin, *Commentaries: Genesis*. Trans I. J. King, 2 vols, Vol 1, Edinburgh: Calvin Translation Soc, 1843.

———. *Commentaries, Psalms*, Vol.4, Grand Rapids, Michigan; Baker Book House.

———. *Institutes of the Christian Religion*. Ed. J. T. McNeill, trans. F. L. Battles, The Library of Christian Classics, 2 vols, Vols.XX, XXI. Philadelphia: Westminster Press, 1960, Vols.1 & 2.

———. Preface to Olivétan's New Testament, *The Library of Christian Classics* Vol.XXIII Calvin: Commentaries, London: SCM Press, 1958, 58–73.

Carr, B. J. and Rees, M. J. "The Anthropic Principle and the Structure of the Physical World". *Nature*, 278 (1979): 605–12.

Carter, B. "Large Number Coincidences and the Anthropic Principle in Cosmology," in M. S. Longair, (ed), *Confrontation of Cosmological Theories with Observational Data*. Holland, Dordrecht: Reidel, 1974.

Cobb, J. B. *Is it too late? A Theology of Ecology*. Beverly Hills, CA: Bruce, 1962.

Collins, F. S. *The Language of God: A Scientist Presents Evidence for Belief*. New York: Simon & Schuster, 2007.

Crowe, M. J. "A History of the Extraterrestrial Life Debate". *Zygon* 32 (1997): 147–62.

———. *The Extraterrestrial Life Debate, 1750–1900*. New York: Dover Publications, 1999.

Darling, D. "On Creating Something From Nothing". *New Scientist*, 151 (1996): 49

Darwin, C. *The Origin of Species*. London: John Murray, 1859; also cited as Darwin. C. *The Origin of Species*. London: Penguin Books, 1985.

———. *The Descent of Man*. London: John Murray, 1871.

Bibliography 163

Darwin, F. *The Life and Letters of Charles Darwin.* 2 vols. (London, 1887), later published in New York by Appleton & Co. in 1898. See also: www.pages.britishlibrary,net/ charles.darwin/texts/ letters/letters2_02html.

———. and Seward, A. C. *More Letters of Charles Darwin.* New York: Appleton, 1903. See also: www.pages.britishlibrary,net/charles.darwin/texts/letters/letters1_fm.html

Davies, P. C. W. *The Mind of God: Science and the Search for Ultimate Meaning.* New York: Simon & Schuster Ltd., 1992.

Davies, P. and Adams, P. *The Big Questions.* Melbourne: Penguin Books Australia, 1996.

———. *More Hard Questions.* Sydney: ABC Books, 1998.

———. "Biological Determinism, Information Theory, and the Origin of Life". in Steven Dick (ed.) *Many Worlds.* Philadelphia and London: Templeton Foundation Press, 2000, 15–28.

Dawkins, R. *The Selfish Gene.* Oxford: Oxford University Press, 1976.

———. *The Blind Watchmaker: Why the Evidence of Evolution reveals a Universe without Design.* New York: W.W. Norton & Co., 1986.

———. *River Out of Eden.* London: Phoenix, 1995.

———. *Climbing Mount Improbable.* New York: W.W. Norton & Co., 1996.

———. *The God Delusion.* Boston, MA: Houghton Mifflin, 2006.

De Duve, C. "Lessons of Life" in Steven Dick (ed.) *Many Worlds.* Philadelphia and London: Templeton Foundation Press, 2000, 3–11.

Desmond, A. and Moore, J. *Darwin.* London: Penguin Books, 1991.

Dick, S. J. "Cosmotheology: Theological Implications of the New Universe," in Steven Dick (ed.) *Many Worlds.* Philadelphia and London: Templeton Foundation Press, 2000, 191–10.

Dirac, P. "The Evolution of the Physicist's Picture of Nature". *Scientific American*, 208 (1963): 45–53.

Dostoevsky, F. *The Brothers Karamozov.* Ed. M. Komroff, trans. C.Garnett, New York: Random House, 1996.

Drake, S. (tr.) *Discoveries and Opinions of Galileo.* New York: Doubleday, 1957.

Draper, J. W. *History of the Conflict between Religion and Science.* London: Henry S. King, 1875.

Duff, M. J. (ed.) *The World in Eleven dimensions: Super-gravity, super-membranes and M-Theory.* Philadelphia, PA.: IOP Publishing, 1999.

Durant, J. (ed.) *Darwinism and Divinity.* Oxford: Blackwell, 1985.

Dyson, F. *Disturbing the Universe.* New York: Harper & Row, 1979.

———. *Infinite in All Directions.* New York: Harper & Row, 1988.

Eccles, J. C. *The Human Mystery.* London: Routledge and Kegan Paul, 1984.

Edgar, B. "Order and Catastrophe: Science and Religion in Australia, 1828". *Pacific Journal of Theology and Science*, 1, (2000): 21–28.

Edwards, D. "Extraterrestrial Life and Jesus Christ". *Pacific Journal of Theology and Science* 1, (2000): 12–20.

Emerton, N. "Arguments for the existence of God from nature and science," in M. Rae, H. Regan, and J. Stenhouse (eds), *Science and Theology: Questions at the Interface.* Edinburgh: T&T Clark, 1994, 72–86.

Eigen, M. *Steps Towards Life.* trans. P. Woolley, Oxford: Oxford University Press, 1992.

Einstein, A. "Science and Religion," *Ideas and Opinions.* Ed. Carl Seelig, New York, Random House, 1988, 36–39.

Einstein, A. "Physics and Reality," *Ideas and Opinions*. Ed. Carl Seelig, New York: Random House, 1988, 290–322.

Fantoli, A. *Galileo: For Copernicanism and for the Church*. Trans. B. V. Coyne, 2nd ed. Vatican Observatory Foundation, 1996.

Fee, G. D. *Paul, the Spirit, and the People of God*. Peabody, MA: Hendrickson, 1996.

Feinberg, G. and Shapiro, R. *Life Beyond Earth: The Intelligent Earthling's Guide to Life in the Universe*. New York: William Morrow, (an imprint of HarperCollins), 1980.

Ferris, T. *The Whole Shebang: A State-of-the-Universe(s) Report*. London: Phoenix, 1998.

Fiddes, P. S. *Participating in God: A Pastoral Doctrine of the Trinity*. London:Darton, Longman and Todd, 2000.

Fox, S. and Dose, K. *Molecular Evolution and the Origin of Life*. New York: Marcel Dekker, 1977.

Freddoso, A. J. "The Openness of God: A Reply to William Hasker," at: http://www.opentheism.org/freddoso.htm

Galilei, G. *Dialogue Concerning the Two Chief World Systems – Ptolemaic and Copernican*, trans. S. Drake, Berkeley, CA: University of California Press, 1953.

Gilkey, L. *Religion and the Scientific Future*. San Fanscisco: Harper, 1970.

Gingerich, O. "Is There Design and Purpose in the Universe?" in John F. Haught (ed.) *Science and Religion: In Search of Comic Purpose*. Washington, DC: Georgetown University Press, 2000, 121–32.

Goodenough, U. *The Sacred Depths of Nature*. New York; Oxford: Oxford University Press, 1998.

Gould, S. J. *Ever Since Darwin*. New York: Norton, 1979.

———. *Dinosaur in a Haystack: Reflections in Natural History*. London: Johnathan Cape, 1996.

———. *Rocks of Ages: Science and Religion in the Fullness of Life*, New York: The Ballantyne Publishing Group, 1999.

Graham, L. R. *Science and Philosophy in the Soviet Union*. New York: Knopf, 1972.

Greene, B. R. *The Elegant Universe: Super-strings, Hidden Dimensions, and the Quest for the Ultimate Theory*. New York: Norton, 1999.

Griffin, D. R. *Unsnarling the World-Knot: Consciousness, Freedom and the Mind-Body Problem*. Berkeley, CA: University of California Press, 1998.

Gross, P. R. and Levitt, N., *The Academic Left and its Quarrels with Science*. Baltimore: Johns Hopkins University Press, 1998.

———. Levitt, N., and Lewis, M. W. (eds.) *The Flight from Science and Reason*. Baltimore: Johns Hopkins University Press, 1997.

Harris, S. *The End of Faith*. New York: W.W. Norton, 2004.

———. *Letter to a Christian Nation*. New York: A. A. Knopf, 2006.

Hartshorne, C. *Man's Vision of God*. Chicago: Willet Clark, 1941.

———. "Panpsychism," in V. Ferm (ed.), *A History of Philosophical Systems*. New York: Rider and Company, 1950, 442–53.

Hawkes, N. J. *An apology for the scientific credibility of faith*. DMin Thesis, Australian College of Theology, 2004.

Hawking, S. W. *A Brief History of Time: From the Big Bang to Black Holes*. London and New York: Bantam, 1988.

———, and Mlodinow, L. *The Grand Design*. New York, Bantam, 2010.

Heisenberg, W. *Physics and Beyond*. New York: Harper and Row, 1971.

Helm, P. (ed.) "John Calvin and Moses Maimonides on Divine Accommodation". *Referring to God*. Surrey, U.K.: Curzon Press, 1999.

———. "Divine Timeless Eternity," in Gregory E. Ganssle (ed.), *Four Views: God and Time*. Downers Grove, Ill: InterVarsity Press, 2001, 28-60.

Hess, P. J. "'God's Two Books': Revelation, Theology Natural Science in the Christian West," in: *Interdisciplinary perspectives on cosmology and biological evolution*, H. D. Regan, M. Worthing (eds.), Adelaide, Australian Theological Forum, 2002, 19-49.

Hick, J. *Evil and the Love of God*. San Francisco, CA.: Harper and Row, 1966.

Horgan J. "Pinning Down Inflation". *Scientific American* 276 (June 1997): 17-19.

Hoyle, F. *The Nature of the Universe*. Oxford, Blackwell, 1950.

———. "Hoyle On Evolution". *Nature* 294 (November 12, 1981):105.

———. "The Universe: Past and Present Reflections". *Engineering and Science* (November, 1981): 8-12.

———. "The Universe: Past and Present Reflections". *Annual Review of Astronomy and Astrophysics* 20 (1982): 135.

Hubble, E. *The Realm of the Nebulae*. New Haven, Connecticut: Yale University Press, 1936.

Huse, S. M. *The Collapse of Evolution*. 3rd edition, Grand Rapids, MI: Baker Book House, 1998.

Hyers, C. *The Meaning of Creation: Genesis, and Modern Science*, Atlanta, Georgia: John Knox Press, 1984.

Jantzen, G. M. *God's World, God's Body*. Philadelphia: Westminster Press, 1984.

Jastrow, R. *God and the Astronomers*. New York: W.W. Norton, 1978.

Jeans, J. H. *The Growth of Physical Science*. Cambridge: Cambridge University Press, 1947.

———. *Physics and Philosophy*. Cambridge: Cambridge University Press, 1948.

Kaldor, P. and Powell, R. *Views from the Pews*. National Church Life Survey, Adelaide: Openbook Publishers, 1995.

Kendrick, T. D. *The Lisbon Earthquake*. London: Methuen & Co. Ltd., 1956.

Keynes, R. *Annie's Box*. London: Fourth Estate, 2001.

Koertge, N. (ed.) *A House Built on Sand: Exposing Postmodernist Myths About Science*. New York and Oxford: Oxford University Press, 1998.

Küppers, B. O. "The World of Biological Complexity; Origin and Evolution of Life," in Steven Dick (ed.) *Many Worlds*. Philadelphia and London: Templeton Foundation Press, 2000, 31-43.

LaHaye, T. and Noebel, D. A. *Mind Siege: The Battle for the Truth in the New Millennium*. Nashville, TN: Word Publishing, 2000.

Lamb, M. *Solidarity with Victims: Toward a Theology of Social Transformation*. New York: Crossroad Publishing Co., 1982.

Larson, E. J. and Witham, L., "Scientists are still keeping the faith," *Nature* 386 (1997): 435-36.

———. "Leading scientists still reject God," *Nature* 394 (1998): 313.

Le Conte, J. *Religion and Science*. New York: D. Appleton and Company, 1902.

Lederman, L. with Teresi, D. *The God Particle: If the Universe Is the Answer, What is the Question?* New York: Bantam Doubleday, 1993.

Leibniz, G. *Philosophical Writings*. Ed G. Parkinson, trans Mary Morris, London: Dent, 1973.

Leslie, J. *Universes*. London; New York: Routledge, 1989.

Leslie, J. "Intelligent Life in Our Universe," in Steven Dick (ed.) *Many Worlds*. Philadelphia and London: Templeton Foundation Press, 2000, 119–32.
Lewis, C. S. *Miracles, A Preliminary Study*. London: Geoffrey Bes, 1947.
Litchfield, H. (ed.) *Emma Darwin: A Century of Family Letters, 1792–1896*. 2 vols, Vol 1, New York: D. Appleton and Co., 1915.
Lorenz, E. N. "Deterministic non-periodic flow," *Journal of the Atmospheric Sciences* 20 (1963): 130–41.
Lovelock, J. E. *Gaia: A new look at life on Earth*. Oxford: Oxford University Press, 1979.
Luther, M. Werke, Weimarer: Ausgabe, 48, 1927.
———. *Luther's Works*. Ed. & trans T. G. Tappert, 55 vols, Vols 52, 54, Philadelphia: Fortress, 1965.
MacKay, D. *Human Science and Human Dignity*: London Lectures in Contemporary Christianity. London: Hodder and Stoughton, 1979.
Matrisciana, C. and Oakland, R. *The Evolution Conspiracy*. Eugene, Oregon: Harvest House, 1991.
McKay, C. P. "Astrobiology: The Search for Life Beyond the Earth," in Steven Dick (ed.) *Many Worlds*. Philadelphia and London: Templeton Foundation Press, 2000, 45–58.
Mayr, E. *Toward a New Philosophy of Biology*. Cambridge: Harvard University Press, 1988.
Medawar, P. *The Limits of Science*. Oxford: Oxford University Press, 1984.
———. *Reformation Thought: An Introduction*. 2nd ed. Oxford: Blackwell, 1993.
McGrath, A. E. *The Foundations of Dialogue in Science and Religion*. Oxford: Blackwell, 1998.
———. *Science & Religion: An introduction*. Oxford: Blackwell, 1999.
McMullin, E. "How Should Cosmology Relate to Theology?" in A. R. Peacocke, (ed.) *The Sciences and Theology in the Twentieth Century*, London: Oriel Press, 1981, 1757.
———. "Life and Intelligence Far from Earth: Formulating Theological Issues," in Steven Dick (ed.) *Many Worlds*. Philadelphia and London: Templeton Foundation Press, 2000, 151–75.
Miele, F. "Darwin's Dangerous Disciple: An Interview with Richard Dawkins," *Skeptic* 3 (1995): 80–85.
Miller, K. R. "Life's Grand Design." *Technology Review* 92 (Feb./March 1994): 24–32.
———. *Finding Darwin's God: A Scientist's Search for Common Ground Between God and Evolution*. New York: Perennial, an imprint of HarperCollins, 1999.
———. "The Flagellum Unspun: The Collapse of 'Irreducible Complexity,'" in W. A. Dembski & M. Ruse, (eds.) *Debating Design: From Darwin to DNA*. New York: Cambridge University Press, 2004: 81–97.
Monod, J. *Chance and Necessity*. Trans. A. Wainhouse, London: Collins, 1972.
Moore, A. "The Christian Doctrine of God," in C. Gore (ed.) *Lux Mundi*, 12th ed. London: John Murray, 1891.
Morris, H. M. *The Twilight of Evolution*. 2nd edition, NorthSantee, CA: Institute for Creation Research, 1998.
Mosse, C. *The Ancient World at Work*. London: Chatto & Windus, 1969.
Murphy, N. C. "Relocating Theology and Science in a Postmodern Age". *CTNS Bulletin* 7.
Newbigin, L. *Foolishness to the Greeks*. London: SPCK, 1986.
O'Donovan, L. J. *A World of Grace: An Introduction to the Themes and Foundations of Karl Rahner's Theology*. New York: Seabury Press, 1984.
Osborn, H. F. *From the Greeks to Darwin*. New York: Charles Scribner's Sons, 1929.

Otis, G. *Transformations: A documentary.* (video), Seattle, WA: The Sentinel Group, 1999.
———. *Transformations II: The Glory Spreads.* (video), Seattle, WA: The Sentinel Group, 2001.
Padgett, A. G. "Eternity As Relative Timelessness," in G. E. Ganssle (ed.), *Four Views: God and Time.* Downers Grove, Ill: InterVarsity Press, 2001, 92–110.
Paine, T. *The Age of Reason* (1793), in E. Foner, (ed.) *Thomas Paine: Collected Writings.* New York: Library of America, 1995.
Pannenberg, W. "Theological Questions to Scientists," in A. R. Peacocke, (ed.) *The Sciences and Theology in the Twentieth Century.* London: Oriel Press, 1981, 3–16.
Paley, W. *Natural Theology.* Revised and annotated edition, Edinburgh: Chambers, 1849.
Paley, W. *Works.* Ed. E. Paley, 6 vols. London: Rivington, 1830.
Paul, P. (John Paul II, - Pope), message to George V. Coyne, *Physics, Philosophy, and Theology: A Common Quest for Understanding.* R. J. Russell, W. R. Stoeger, SJ, and G. V. Coyne, S. J. (eds), Vatican City State: Vatican Observatory, 1988. M1-M14.
Pascal, B. *Pensées.* (1670) trans. W. F. Trotter, New York: Modern Library, 1941.
Peacocke, A. R. (ed.) *The Sciences and Theology in the Twentieth Century.* London: Oriel Press, 1981.
———. *Intimations of Reality.* University of Nôtre Dame Press, 1984.
———. *Theology for a Scientific Age: Being and Becoming - Natural, Divine, and Human.* London: SCM and Minneapolis: Fortress Press, 1993.
———. *God and Science: A Quest for Christian Credibility.* London: SCM, 1996.
———. "The Challenge and Stimulus of the Epic of Evolution to Theology" in Steven Dick (ed.) *Many Worlds.* Philadelphia and London: Templeton Foundation Press, 2000, 89–17.
———. "The Cost of New Life," in John Polkinghorne (ed.) *The Work of Love: Creation as Kenosis.* Grand Rapids, MI.: Eerdmans, 2001, 21–42.
Pennock, R. T. *Tower of Babel: The Evidence Against New Creationism.* Cambridge, MA: The MIT Press, 2000.
Peters, E. "Theology and Science: Where are We?" *Zygon* 31 (1996): 325–31.
Peterson, I. *Newton's Clock: Chaos in the Solar System.* New York: MacMillan, 1993.
Pinnock, C. H. "God's sovereignty in today's world". *Theology Today* (Princeton Theological Library: N.J.) 53 (1996): 15f.
———. *Most Moved Mover: A Theology of God's Openness.* Carlisle, U.K.: Paternoster Press, 2001.
Polkinghorne, J. *Reason and Reality: The Relationship between Science and Theology.* London: SPCK, 1991.
———. *Science and Christian Belief.* London: SPCK, 1994.
———. *Quarks, Chaos, and Christianity.* London: Triangle, SPCK, 1994.
———. *Scientists as Theologians.* London: SPCK, 1996.
———. *Science and Theology: An Introduction.* London: SPCK, 1998.
———. *Belief in God in an Age of Science.* Yale University Press, 1998.
———. "Kenotic Creation and Divine Action," in John Polkinghorne (ed.) *The Work of Love: Creation as Kenosis.* Grand Rapids, MI: Eerdmans, 2001, 90–106.
Polanyi, M. *Personal Knowledge: Towards a Post-Critical Philosophy.* London: Routledge & Kegan Paul, 1958.
Puccetti, R. *Persons: A Study of Possible Moral Agents in the Universe.* London: Macmillan, 1968.

Puddefoot, J. C. *Logic and Affirmation: Perspectives in Mathematics and Theology.* Edinburgh: Scottish Academic Press, 1987.

Rahner, K. *Foundations of Christian Faith.* New York: Crossroad, 1978.

———. "Natural Science and Reasonable Faith". *Theological Investigations* XXI, New York: Seabury Press, (1988).

Rees, M. *Before the Beginning: Our Universe and Others.* London: Simon and Schuster, 1997.

———. *Just Six Numbers: The Deep Forces that Shape the Universe.* New York: Basic Books (Perseus Group), 2000.

Rennie, J. "15 Answers to Creationist Nonsense". *Scientific American* 287 (2002): 62–69.

Rolston, H. "Science, Religion and the Future" in W. M. Richardson and W. J.Wildman (eds) *Religion and Science: History, Method, and Dialogue.* London and New York: Routledge, 1996.

Russell, R. J. "How the Heaven's Have Changed". *CTNS Bulletin* (Berkeley, CA) 19 (1999): 33–10.

———. "Intelligent Life in the Universe: Philosophical and Theological Issues". (working draft) Center for Theology and the Natural Sciences, Berkeley, U.S.A. www.ictp.trieste.it/~chelaf/lecture.html

Stephens, W. P. *The Theology of Huldrych Zwingli.* Oxford:Clarendon Press, 1986.

Smolin, L. "Our Relationship to the Universe" in Steven Dick (ed.) *Many Worlds.* Philadelphia and London: Templeton Foundation Press, 2000 79–86.

Sokal, A. "Transgressing the Boundaries: Toward a Transformative Hermeneutics of Quantum Gravity" *Social Text,* Spring-Summer, nos. 46–47, (1996): 217–52.

———. "A physicist experiments with cultural studies". *Lingua Franca* (May-June, 1996): 62–64.

———. and Bricmont, J. *Intellectual Impostures: Postmodern Philosophers' abuse of science.* London: Profile Books, 1998.

Stark, R. and Finke, R. *Acts of Faith: Explaining the Human Side of Religion.* Berkeley, CA.: University of California Press, 2000.

Stenhouse, J. Response to Norma Emerton's paper "Arguments for the existence of God from nature and science" in M. Rae; H. Regan and J. Stenhouse (eds.), *Science and Theology: Question at the Interface.* Edinburgh: T&T Clark, 1994, 87–100.

Sullivan, W. *We Are Not Alone.* Revised edition, New York: Penguin Books, 1993.

Tappert, T. G. (trans. & ed.) *Luther's Works.* 54, Philadelphia: Fortress, 1967.

Tarter, J. C. "SETI and the Religions of the Universe," in Steven Dick (ed.) *Many Worlds.* Philadelphia and London: Templeton Foundation Press, 2000, 143–49.

Taylor, H. S. (ed.) *Newton's Philosophy of Nature: Selections from his Writings.* New York: Hafner, 1953.

Temple, F. "The Present Relations of Science to Religion": A Sermon Preached on July 1, 1860 before the University of Oxford, referred to in Brooke, J. and Cantor, G. *Reconstructing Nature: The Engagement of Science and Religion.* Edinburgh: T&T Clark, 1988, 36.

Tertullian, *Contra Marcionem* I.xviii. (See: www.gnosis.org/library/ter_marc1.htm).

Teilhard de Chardin, P. *Towards the Future.* trans. Rene Hague, London: Collins, 1975.

Tillich, P. *Systematic Theology.* 3 vols, Chicago: Univ. of Chicago Press, 1951-1963.

Thomson, W. (Lord Kelvin), "The Structure of Matter and the Unity of Science," in G. Basalla, W. Colman, and R. H. Kargon (eds) *Victorian Science: A Self-Portrait from the Presidential Addresses of the British Association for the advancement of Science.* New York: Doubleday, 1970, 98–128.

Torrance, T. F. "God and the Contingent World". *Zygon* 14 (1979): 329–48.
———. "Divine and Contingent Order," in A. R. Peacocke, (ed.) *The Sciences and Theology in the Twentieth Century*. Stocksfield, U.K.: Oriel Press, 1981, 8197.
———. *Divine and Contingent Order*. Oxford University Press, 1981.
———. *Preaching Christ Today; The Gospel and Scientific Thinking*. Grand Rapids, Michigan: Eerdmans, 1994.
Toulmin, S. *The Return to Cosmology: Postmodern Science and the Theology of Nature*. Berkeley; University of California Press, 1985.
Trefil, J. *The Dark side of the Universe*. New York: Scribner's, 1988.
Trimble, V. "Cosmology: Man's Place in the Universe". *American Scientist* 65 (1977): 76–86.
Wade, R. "God and the Future: Examining The Open View of God". Richardson, TX: Probe Ministries, 2000. (See also:http://www.probe.org/docs/openview.html).
Watts, F. (ed.) *Science Meets Faith: Theology and Science in Conversation*. London: SPCK, 1998.
Wedgwood, B. and H. *The Wedgwood Circle*. Westfield, N.J.: Eastview, 1980.
Weinberg, S. *The First Three Minutes: A Modern View of the Origin of the Universe*. New York: Basic Books, 1977.
Wells, J. A., *Icons of Evolution: Science or Myth?* Washington, DC: Regenery Publishing, 2000.
———. "The Universe as Home for Man," O. Gingerich (ed.) *The Nature of Scientific Discovery*. Washington: Smithsonian Institute Press, 1975, 261–96.
Wheeler, J. A. *At Home in the Universe*. New York: Springer Verlag, 1992.
White, A. D. A *History of the Warfare of Science with Theology in Christendom*. New York: D. Appleton and Co., 1896.
Whitehead, A. N. *Process and Reality: An Essay in Cosmology*. Cambridge, Cambridge University Press, 1929.
———. *Process and Reality*. Ed. D. R. Griffin and D. W. Sherburne, (corrected ed.). New York: Free Press, 1978.
Wheatley, G. H."Constructivist Perspectives on Science and Mathematics Learning". *Science Education* 1 (1991): 9–21.
Wilson, E. O. *Sociobiology: The New Synthesis*. Cambridge: Harvard University Press, 1975.
Woodall, D. L. "The Relationship between Science and Scripture in the Thought of Robert Boyle," *Perspectives on Science and Christian Faith* 49 (1997): 32–39.
Worthing, M. *God, Creation and Contemporary Physics*. Minneapolis: Fortress Press, 1996.
———. "Science and Theology – An Historical Overview". *Pacific Journal of Theology and Science* 1 (2000): 5–11.
van Huyssteen, J. W. *Duet or Duel? Theology and Science in a Postmodern World*. London: SCM, 1998.1
van Huyssteen, W. J. *Theology and the Justification of Faith*. Grand Rapids, MI: Eerdmans, 1989.
Note: Huyssteen J. W. and Huyssteen W. J. (see above) are the same person listed with different initials in each publication.
von Glasersfeld, E. "Cognition, Construction of Knowledge, and Teaching". *Synthese* 80 (1989): 121–40.
von Hoerner, S. "The Likelihood of Interstellar Colonization and the Absence of Evidence," in Zuckerman B, and Hart, M. H. *Extraterrestrials, Where Are They?* (2nd ed.) Cambridge University Press, 1995, 29–31.

www.ingramcontent.com/pod-product-compliance
Lightning Source LLC
Chambersburg PA
CBHW050845160426
43192CB00011B/2158